LEGENDS OF WARFARE
AVIATION

The 406th Fighter Group

P-47s over Europe in World War II

STEVEN A. BRANDT, PHD

SCHIFFER MILITARY

4880 Lower Valley Road   Atglen, PA 19310

Designed by Justin Watkinson
Type set in Impact/Minion Pro/Univers LT Std

ISBN: 978-0-7643-6652-9
Printed in India

Published by Schiffer Publishing, Ltd.
4880 Lower Valley Road
Atglen, PA 19310
Phone: (610) 593-1777; Fax: (610) 593-2002
Email: Info@schifferbooks.com
Web: www.schifferbooks.com

For our complete selection of fine books on this and related subjects, please visit our website at www.schifferbooks.com. You may also write for a free catalog.

Schiffer Publishing's titles are available at special discounts for bulk purchases for sales promotions or premiums. Special editions, including personalized covers, corporate imprints, and excerpts, can be created in large quantities for special needs. For more information, contact the publisher.

We are always looking for people to write books on new and related subjects. If you have an idea for a book, please contact us at proposals@schifferbooks.com.

Dedication

To the men of the 406th Fighter Group and their families. They wrote this story with their sweat, tears, and blood.

Courtesy of Pima Air and Space Museum

Contents

Preface

This book is the first stand-alone history of the 406th Fighter Group that has ever been published by a major publisher. Aside from the official USAAF histories of the group and its three squadrons, only a few yearbook-like histories intended for group members and their families were ever published. This contrasts with dozens of books written about famous units such as the 56th, 78th, and 353rd Fighter Groups.

That is not to say the group has been neglected by historians or, in particular, artists and modelers. The superb photos made from color slides taken by group members John Quincy and Stanley Wyglendowski ensured that the group, its aircraft, and its personnel held prominent places in many histories of the Republic P-47 Thunderbolt and the 9th Air Force. These, in turn, led to popularity with manufacturers and model builders of plastic and die-cast model kits, and ultimately, to a 406th Fighter Group P-47 appearing on a United States postage stamp.

Unfortunately, the information available in the most-popular photos was incomplete. This led to misunderstandings and assumptions that were incorrect. This book will correct those errors by adding significantly to the information and photo documentation of the aircraft in question. This expanded documentation will also show how the markings on some aircraft evolved over the course of the 406th Fighter Group's year in combat.

This book will also add to the reader's understanding of how the group and its squadrons, flights, and individual aircraft crews, starting with aircraft usually supplied in standard theater ID markings, decorated their aircraft and added to those decorations from time to time. It will also highlight the reasons for mismatched color schemes, including olive-drab wings and tails, that appeared on some of the aircraft, testimony to the incredible ingenuity and tireless effort by dedicated ground crews who kept the 406th Fighter Group in the air. This is done to honor the men who wrote the story in their blood and sweat, and to inspire another generation of artists and model builders to also honor those men with more-accurate representations of those wartime experiences.

Steven A. Brandt, PhD
Colorado Springs, 2022

Acknowledgments

Final approach. *Digital copy from AAF film held by US National Archives, licensed by criticalpast.com*

The author is extremely grateful to the past members of the 406th Fighter Group (FG) who have taken time over the years to tell the stories recorded in this book. This began with the author's own father, Fred V. Brandt, who told stories as he worked with his son on the farm in Iowa. It continued with Brandt's squadron mates from the 512th Fighter Squadron (FS), whom the author met at the 406th Fighter Group reunions, which began in 1981 and continued through 2007. In particular, Richard Dean and William Cunningham took time to tell stories and share photos.

The most-recent and in some ways most-inspiring conversations have occurred since 2010 with Ernie Sprouse, Jack Yarger, and John Bronson. Though advanced in years, these gentlemen all have vivid memories of their World War II experiences, and they are happy to share them. Thanks also to David, Anna, and Lori, who are caregivers for these men and who helped set up the visits and phone calls.

Most of the photos in this book have never been published by a major publisher before. They were obtained from the 406th Fighter Group World War II Memorial Association's excellent archive, maintained at the Pima Air and Space Museum (PASM) in Tucson, Arizona. Many thanks are due to Bob Campbell, president of the association, and to John Bezoski and the rest of the PASM staff for their assistance in making these photos available. The archive holds records and photos contributed by many veterans who were members of the 406th FG in World War II and by their families. As such, it is a priceless treasure.

Some photos are of relatively low quality. They are included because they show scenes not documented in any other way. Only a few group members had really good cameras at the time. The majority were fixed-focus jobs with poor-quality lenses, so the photos are often fuzzy and blurred. Other lower-quality photos were extracted from movies held by PASM and by the US National Archives. Again, they are the only documentation available of specific information, so they are included.

It is the stated purpose of this book to set the record straight where possible. Certainly, some of the major misunderstandings resulting from limited photo documentation available until now are easily corrected by the photos in this work, but many questions are still left unanswered. A little detective work and careful cross-referencing of the various sources can sometimes turn up new information or conclusions. But inevitably, there will still be errors in this book. Please know that every effort has been made to avoid this. These brave men deserve no less.

Introduction

Photo from AAF film crew via US National Archives

A history of an American fighter group in World War II Europe is a story of men and machines in a struggle against a powerful, resourceful, and battle-hardened enemy. It is a story of skill pitted against skill and technology pitted against technology, but most of all, courage and grit pitted against courage and grit. The story of the 406th Fighter Group in World War II is all of these things and more. It is an incredible story of men overcoming massive obstacles to defeat the most successful military machine that had ever existed at that point in history.

The standard image of a fighter plane in World War II Europe is one of a pristine prima donna made of polished metal and Plexiglas, flying from a paved runway or grassy field into the bright-blue skies of jolly old England. The P-47s of the 406th Fighter Group were something different. They were battle-scarred kickboxers, flying from muddy metal-mat runways into murky skies, slugging it out with the Luftwaffe and Wehrmacht in a hail of flak and flying debris. It is this image that should come through clearly in this book. Most of the aircraft described herein were shot down. Those that survived were repaired using parts from the scrap pile, useful remnants of planes too badly damaged to repair. The evidence of those repairs is seen throughout the book, olive-drab badges of courage that tell their own story.

The men in this history deserve more attention than there is room to give them. Only a few of the many experiences can be told in the space available. Those stories that are told herein were chosen to give a flavor of all the stories, all the experiences that make up the fascinating history of the 406th Fighter Group in World War II.

Flightline transportation. *Courtesy of Pima Air and Space Museum*

Tents and foxholes. *Courtesy of Pima Air and Space Museum*

CHAPTER 1
Origins

Congaree Army Air Base, Columbia, South Carolina, October 1943. *Courtesy of Pima Air and Space Museum*

The unit that was to become the 406th Fighter Group was activated on March 1, 1943, by General Order 28, Headquarters Key Field, Meridian, Mississippi, as the 406th Bomb Group (Dive), under the command of Lt. Col. Bryan B. Harper. The *406th Occupier* newspaper's historical edition records the following:

It was composed of the 628th, 629th, 630th, and 631st Squadrons and was a part of the III Air Support Command, Birmingham, Ala., and the III Air Force, Tampa, Florida. In April and May 1943 all personnel attended AAF School of Applied Tactics, Orlando, Florida, for the Air Support course. In June and July, the organization was brought to fifty percent of full strength and received its first planes: one A-35, one A-24, and one BC-1 per squadron. This period was one of organization, training of key personnel and acquiring equipment.

In August, 1943 the group was reorganized and redesignated the 406th Fighter Bomber Group composed of the 512th, 513th and 514th Squadrons and transferred to command of the III Fighter Command, Drew Field, Tampa, Florida. In September 1943, a change of station was ordered and the group moved to Congaree Army Air Base, Columbia, South Carolina. By October 1, 1943, the organization was to full strength in ground personnel and half strength in flying personnel, had received Bell P-39 aircraft, and had begun a combat readiness-training program prescribed by the III Fighter Command.

A tactical inspection at the end of October identified inadequate fighter time of all pilots. Though experienced in dive-bombers, they averaged less than a hundred hours in fighters. All flying personnel were reassigned. Several pilots released from the unit at this time eventually rejoined it in England. It was a grand reunion when they arrived as replacement pilots at their respective squadrons.

Lt. Col. Anthony V. Grossetta assumed command of the group from Lt. Col. Harper on November 6, 1943. Col. Grossetta had flown P-36s and P-40s in Alaska during 1941 and 1942, so he brought with him practical experience in wartime fighter operations and combat. On December 1, 1943, the group received new flying personnel and Republic P-47 Thunderbolt aircraft. The period from December 1, 1943, to March 1, 1944, was spent in gunnery, dive-bombing, formation, and mission training. This period also saw intense preparation for overseas movement. Movement orders arrived on March 1, 1944. On the thirteenth, the unit proceeded to the port of embarkation.

406th Fighter Bomber Group Douglas A-24 flying over South Carolina. *Courtesy of Pima Air and Space Museum*

406th Fighter Bomber Group Curtiss A-25 at Congaree Army Airfield. *Courtesy of Pima Air and Space Museum*

406th Fighter Bomber Group Bell P-39 at Congaree Army Airfield. *Courtesy of Pima Air and Space Museum*

406th Fighter Bomber Group Republic P-47 at Congaree Army Airfield. *Courtesy of Pima Air and Space Museum*

CHAPTER 2
Ashford

512th FS aircraft parked at ALG 417. *Courtesy of Pima Air and Space Museum*

Advanced Landing Ground 417, Ashford, Kent, UK
April 6, 1944–July 31, 1944

On Monday, March 13, 1944, at 0900, as a band played "Auld Lang Syne," the 406th Fighter Group, thereafter known as shipment number 1404N, entrained for the port of embarkation. Thirty-six hours later they arrived at Camp Shanks, New York. The group immediately established a headquarters and began processing. Security and censorship orientation, equipment checks, records inspections, and physical examinations filled the next four days. When finished, group personnel were released for passes to New York City. Restriction came on March 20, and on the twenty-second, the organization boarded HMT Stirling Castle of the Union Castle Line via Weehawken Ferry. Once again, a band played to add an upbeat and patriotic mood to the process. Early on March 23, *Stirling Castle* sailed for England.

The crossing was uneventful. In the afternoon of April 3, Stirling Castle dropped anchor in Liverpool, and 1404N was the first to debark. Greeted by coffee, doughnuts, and the first sight of bomb damage, the unit boarded a typical tiny English train and started across England for Ashford, Kent. The regular green pattern of the countryside, with neat towns and thousands of chimneys, soon faded into the dark of the English night. The following day at 0700, the train arrived at Ashford. It was met by Lt. Col. Leslie Bratton, Maj. William Merriam, Capt. Jeptha Larkin, and Capt. Irvin Rome. These men had preceded the group by air as the advance party.

A first look at Advanced Landing Ground (ALG) 417 indicated there was plenty to do to become operational. Thanks to the work of the advance party, the minimum initial equipment was on hand so that the many tasks could begin immediately. The next two weeks saw tents pitched, offices set up in trailers and farmhouses,

dispersal areas cleared, and equipment acquired. The group set up its communication systems, established its administrative and operations headquarters, sent its officers off for schools and orientation courses, and acquired supporting and service organizations. A few war-weary P-47s arrived starting on April 13. Limited flying began on the fifteenth. For the rest of the month, many 406th pilots flew with other units to get experience in the theater. By the end of the month, the basic organization was established, most training was done, and the group lacked only more planes and parts to go operational.

The assignment of group pilots to fly with other units brought one staggering loss to the 514th FS. The 514th Squadron commander, Maj. Gene L. Arth, while flying with the 337th Fighter-Bomber Squadron of the 362nd Fighter-Bomber Group on April 22, 1944, was hit by flak while strafing a train. He never pulled out of the dive. On May 3, Capt. Converse B. Kelly was appointed the new commander of the 514th.

The group was assigned to XIX Tactical Air Command (TAC) of the 9th Air Force and flew its first operational sortie on May 9, 1944. Led by Col. Grossetta, the mission was an uneventful sweep northwest of Paris. Another mission the next day went farther north and east. These missions continued until the thirteenth, when the group escorted B-26s. On this escort mission the group encountered enemy aircraft for the first time. Two Bf 109s and two Fw 190s attacked the 513th and shot down Lt. Charles B. Hall in 42-75437. Enemy fire also started a hydraulic-fluid fire in the left wing of 2Lt. Wayne T. Swanbery's plane. The fire blew out as he dove away from the fight, and he was able to return to Ashford.

406th FG aircraft fly over ALG 417 tent city. *Courtesy of Pima Air and Space Museum*

Courtesy of Pima Air and Space Museum

The evolution of the 406th came full circle on May 19, 1944, when the unit, which was originally activated as a dive-bomb group, dive-bombed a marshaling yard at Cambrais. Pilots began their dives at 7,000 feet, with bomb release between 3,500 and 2,000 feet. Three 500 lb. bombs hit a repair shop in the center of the yard, seven more 500-pounders exploded within the yard, and a bridge west of the target was demolished. Not bad for fighter-bombers! This success was an important step in converting the fighter pilots of the 406th into the crack ground-attack pilots they would become.

The next day the group flew into Belgium and western Germany to strafe railroad rolling stock. On ensuing days the marshaling yard at Creil, France; a railroad bridge at St. Germain; and the Cambrais/Epernay airdrome were the targets. Most of the remaining missions entailed the escort of bombers. On the twenty-fourth, the group encountered enemy aircraft again. Four Fw 190s made a pass at the 512th FS and were beaten off with some damage, but no losses on either side. On the twenty-eighth, the group escorted B-17s for the first time. The group continued escort missions for the rest of the month.

For the period, the 406th flew twenty-one combat missions, ranging from four fighter sweeps in the beginning to twelve escorts with four interspersed dive-bombs and one antirail strafing foray. These missions totaled 935 sorties. Col. Grossetta was promoted to full colonel on May 27.

After achieving three kills with pilot Lt. Paul Conger in the 56th FG, 42-75345 spent only two months with the 512th FS. It and pilot Lt. Lyon E. Agee were lost due to flak near Cherbourg on June 22, 1944.

406th FG Unit Emblem

The first of several 512th FS P-47s coded L3-A and named "Old Buzzard Ass." Serial number is not quite readable.

Aircraft from the 514th FS taking off at ALG 417.

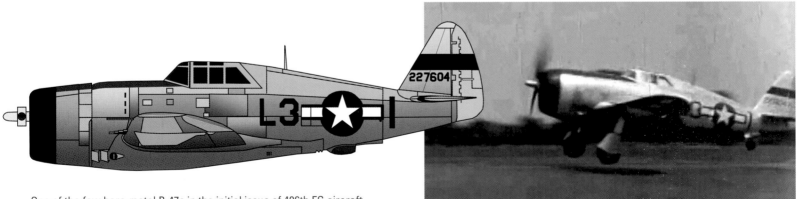

One of the few bare-metal P-47s in the initial issue of 406th FG aircraft, 42-27604, was brought down by flak on June 19, 1944, while being flown by the 512th FS DO, Maj. Weston M. Lennox. He evaded capture and returned to England, then back to the States.

All photos this page courtesy of Pima Air and Space Museum

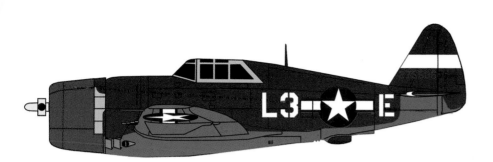

No photos show a 406th FG P-47 with a white nose. Many undoubtedly came from the 8th Air Force with white ID bands on their noses, but all were apparently painted in a squadron color, yellow for the 512th, red for the 513th, and blue for the 514th. Black ID bands were left black. Perhaps this practice stemmed from Col. Grossetta's experience in Alaska.

Most of the group's first aircraft were hand-me-downs from 8th Air Force units. The bubble-canopied P-47D-25RE and later models were just appearing in Europe, so all the initial 406th aircraft were "razorbacks." *All photos this page courtesy of Pima Air and Space Museum.*

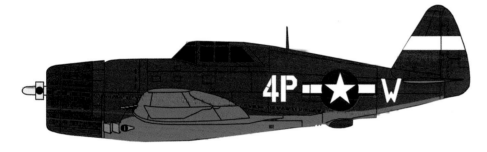

This aircraft and pilot Harry A. Nock were lost in aerial combat on July 4, 1944.

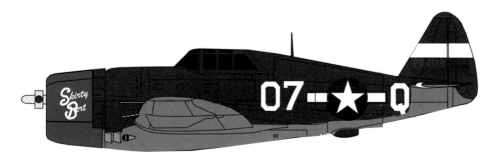

The Thunderbolts assigned to 514th FS commander Maj. Converse B. Kelly were named "Skirty Bert," with aircraft ID code 07-Q, 42-8409, probably the first of these. It and pilot Lt. Merlin E. Isbell were lost in aerial combat on June 10, 1944. He was KIA.

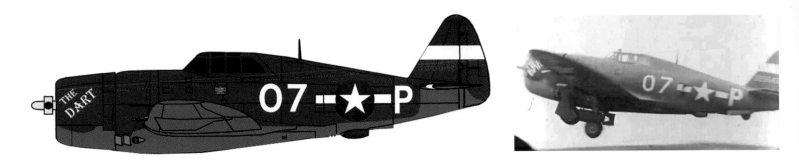

In the hustle to get operational, cowlings that were not painted white were left olive drab and gray, but every white nose was painted a squadron color.

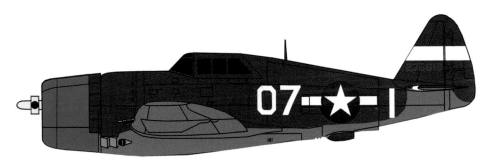

There is no discernible pattern as to why some Thunderbolts had only the first 24 inches of their cowlings painted while others received completely painted cowls.

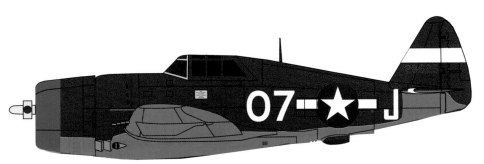

This aircraft and pilot Lt. Lewis A. Burton were lost due to flak on June 17, 1944.

All photos this page courtesy of Pima Air and Space Museum

406h FG mass launch from ALG 417 in May 1944. *All photos this page courtesy of Pima Air and Space Museum*

CHAPTER 3
Invasion

No white noses at ALG 417. *Courtesy of Pima Air and Space Museum*

June 1944

June 1944 was a tense and busy time for the 406th Fighter Group. The first days of the month combined missions of the preinvasion air campaign with planning and preparation for the maximum effort that was coming. The briefing tent was closed to most personnel, aircraft were painted with black-and-white stripes, and everyone wondered, "When?"

On the evening of June 5, to a packed briefing tent, Col. Grossetta, along with the group intelligence officer, Maj. Larkin, and the deputy commander, Lt. Col. Bratton, revealed the plan for the group's part in the invasion. It was a short night. Before dawn, Col. Grossetta led sixteen aircraft off to cover Utah Beach. Heavy clouds made the climb to cruise altitude exciting! The group flew four top-cover missions a day for the next five days as part of Operation Neptune.

Lights had been rigged along the edges of runway 15/33 at Ashford. During one of these predawn mass launches, a taxiing P-47 hooked the lights and ripped up the wiring. In the dark, Lt. Jack Robinson of the 512th drove a jeep to the far end of the runway and pointed its headlights toward the other end. Takeoffs continued, with pilots aiming their planes at the jeep headlights.

After the first week, the group switched from top cover to interdiction. This meant cutting rails, attacking marshaling yards, and strafing anything that moved behind the beachhead. Returning from one of these missions, Capt. Raymond Walsh of the 513th became the first American pilot to shoot down a V-1. He encountered the "buzz bomb" off the coast of England and promptly dispatched it. He was interviewed on a BBC broadcast on June 17.

Each squadron within the 406th had a unique radio call sign: Basher for the 512th, Roscoe for the 513th, and Raider for the 514th. The lead flight in a squadron mission was Red Flight, then Yellow (or White in the 513th), then Blue, and if the squadron put up sixteen planes, the fourth flight was Green Flight. Individual call signs included that plane's number or position within the flight. So, the leader of the 512th FS on a mission was "Basher Red Leader" or "Basher Red One," and the wingman of the second element in the third flight of a 514th FS mission was "Raider Blue Four."

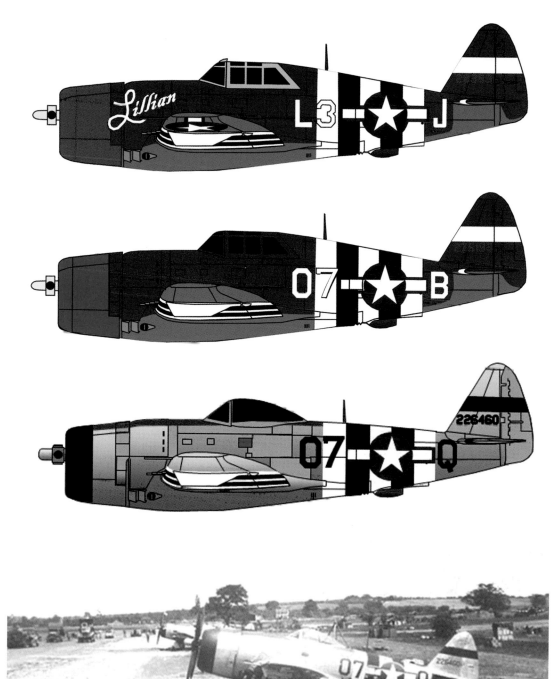

All of the planes assigned to Lt. James C. Brown had the name "Lillian" painted on them, but apparently only 42-8389 was coded L3-J. It was brought down by flak near Cherbourg on June 22, 1944, and pilot Elmer C. Dudolski was MIA. In July, Capt. Jack Bronson was assigned the L3-J code for his aircraft. It is presumed that Brown's new aircraft ID was L3-B.

This P-47 was lost due to flak, along with pilot 2Lt. Bryant L. Cramer, on August 7, 1944.

At some point in June, the group received 12 brand new P-47s with bubble canopies and Hamilton-Standard hydromatic paddle-blade propellers. Four went to each squadron. 42-26460 was probably assigned to 514th FS commander Converse B. Kelly since his aircraft ID code was always 07-Q. At the time of the ceremony shown in the photo the name "Skirty Bert II" had not yet been applied. The photo was taken at ALG 417 in early July 1944. The order to remove the top half of invasion stripes was given on July 6, 1944.

Capt. Kelly leading ceremony at ALG 417.
Courtesy of Pima Air and Space Museum

Aircraft of the 406th FG parked at ALG 417. *Courtesy of Pima Air and Space Museum*

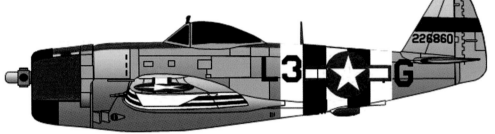

One new bubble-canopied P-47 received in June or July was 42-26860, a P-47D-27RE in bare metal with full black European theater of operations ID bands and invasion stripes. It was coded L3-G. That's Col. Anthony V. Grossetta, 406th FG commander, posing with the aircraft in the photos on this page. The "high rollers" in the unit were usually assigned the individual aircraft ID letter corresponding to the first letter of their last name, so this aircraft was probably assigned to the colonel at the time of the photo. The olive-drab-and-gray cowling panel from an older Thunderbolt is a puzzle. It may have been installed just for the photo to hide some sensitive nose art. This P-47 would become arguably the most famous Thunderbolt in the 406th. But that story will be told in another chapter.

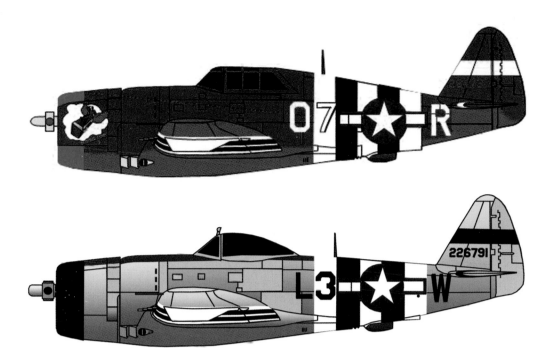

At least 9 P-47s assigned to 1Lt. J.C. Van Bloom carried the ID code 07-R and had the name "BLOOM'S TOMB" painted on them. Most also carried artwork painted by S/Sgt. Sam Mickwee showing a pilot in flight suit riding a winged coffin. There is a good chance the nose art cowling panel on this aircraft was salvaged from BLOOM'S TOMB #1, which bellied in at ALG 417 on June 8, 1944. BLOOM'S TOMB #2, 42-8473 was being flown by Lt. Levitt C. Beck on June 29, 1944, when he shot down an Fw 190 in a head-on pass but was also shot down. Hidden by the French underground, he wrote a diary which eventually was published as a book titled *Fighter Pilot*. Beck was betrayed by a double-agent, captured, sent to the infamous Buchenwald concentration camp, and died there. His diary, hidden in his French hideout, was discovered and mailed to his parents after the war.

The 512th FS lost several directors of operations (DOs or vice commanders) while flying from Ashford. As mentioned earlier, Maj. Weston M. Lennox went down on June 10, 1944. He returned to the squadron after a month behind enemy lines but did not fly in combat again. Lennox was replaced by Capt. Creighton A Smith, who was badly burned in a takeoff accident on July 4, 1944. The next DO was Capt. John W. Mullaney, who was hit by flak while strafing on July 30, 1944, and went straight in, no parachute. Mullaney was flying 42-26791 L3-W, which was undoubtedly one of the new bubble jobs received by the 512th in June. Smith's plane was probably another. The next in line by date of rank to be DO was Capt. Jack Bronson. He managed to break the streak of bad luck and rose to command the 512th during the Battle of the Bulge.

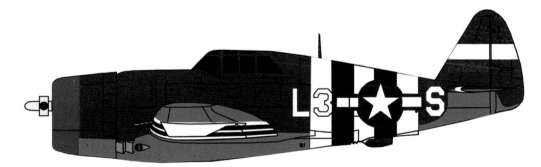

Flying from Ashford, it became increasingly difficult to support the Army on the Continent. As the front lines moved farther east, flying distances got longer and time over the battle got shorter. And getting home with battle damage or low fuel got harder. And 42-76245 made an emergency landing at advanced landing ground A-3, Cardonville, France. It was clear that the 406th FG needed to move across the channel. The 406th was the last 9th AF fighter group to move to France. It may be that this fact caused them to be selected as the first unit to get a powerful new weapon, or it may be that receiving the new weapon delayed their move.

512th FS aircraft parked at ALG 417. *Courtesy of Pima Air and Space Museum*

CHAPTER 4
Rockets!

513th FS aircraft showing rockets and rocket stubs.

July 1944

In early July, the 513th Fighter Squadron began installing and training with the 5-inch, high-velocity aerial rocket (HVAR). This weapon was the first of its kind used on American fighter aircraft in the European theater of operations (ETO). None of the 406th Fighter Group ever used the three-barrel bazooka-type rocket launchers seen on other P-47s. Instead, the HVAR installation consisted of in-line pairs of stubs on which the rockets were mounted, two pairs under each wing, directly below the .50-caliber machine guns.

To start things off, seventeen brand-new, bare-metal, bubble-canopied P-47s arrived already modified to carry the rockets. The other 513th FS Thunderbolts were sent off to the depot at Burtonwood, where they were also modified, while the pilots trained in the new aircraft. The training was done rapidly and without a letup in operational flying. Trainers set up a target on the runway at ALG 417, and 513th pilots in their new planes made repeated practice runs on it. On July 17, 1944, rockets were used in an attack against a marshaling yard at Nevers. The rocket-firing Thunderbolts destroyed no fewer than twenty-five locomotives! The 513th became crack shots with these weapons, killing countless tanks, locomotives, and even a ship! With the hitting power of a 5-inch naval gun, the HVARs made the P-47 even more formidable.

The P-47s of the 512th and 514th Squadrons did not receive this mod. When those squadrons would encounter targets such as tanks that were resistant to their bombs and machine guns, they would call for "rockets" or "Roscoe," the 513th.

513th FS aircraft showing rockets and rocket stubs. *All photos this page courtesy of Pima Air and Space Museum*

513th FS aircraft showing rockets and rocket stubs. *All photos this page courtesy of Pima Air and Space Museum*

Stenciling on body of 5-inch High-Velocity Aerial Rocket (HVAR) seen in 406th FG display at Pima Air and Space Museum. Note low temperature limit.

Stenciling and nose details on 5-inch HVAR in 406th FG display at Pima Air and Space Museum. Impact velocity was 3,000 ft/s.

Courtesy of Pima Air and Space Museum

Elsie with Rockets! *Courtesy of Pima Air and Space Museum*

CHAPTER 5
Normandy

406th FG aircraft taking off from an airstrip on the continent. *AAF photo*

On July 19, the 406th began its journey to join the other 9th AF fighter-bomber units on the Continent. The air echelon proceeded by train and trucks to a staging area near Plymouth, then waited there for a week for further orders. Interdiction of Normandy continued, and the group, with only half of its personnel available in the ground echelon and less than half its equipment, flew four missions a day from ALG 417. During this period of intense activity with reduced resources, the group received its first written commendation for missions on July 23.

The first elements of the air echelon boarded ships on the 23rd. The *406th Occupier* describes their arrival in Normandy: "After an overnight trip across the channel first elements of the air echelon came alongside Omaha beach on July 24, to be followed the next day by the vehicle serials on Liberty ships. . . . On the same day the squadrons back in England were participating in the first of a 2-day saturation attack on enemy lines below St. Lô. In addition the rocket[-]firing aircraft of the 513th Squadron had moved to the continent to operate separately from advanced landing strip A-2. On the morning of the 25th the air echelon started out in search of its assigned air strip in the vicinity of Bayeux, the group flew its part of Operation Cobra again and the Thunderbolts with the secret weapon hunted the hedgerows for enemy tanks."

The air echelon arrived at Strip A-13 near Bayeux, France, by noon of the twenty-fifth. The *406th Occupier* continues: "At first all was confusion but before another day had passed the tents were pitched, areas assigned, and some resemblance of order achieved. In a couple of days the 513th moved down from A-2, Col. Grossetta flew in from the United Kingdom, communications were established with the 70th Fighter Wing and the place was ready to receive airplanes."

Temporary Airfield A-13. Carefully sculpted elm trees bordered the group's first airfield on the Continent. *AAF photo*

Temporary Airfield A-14. Located near Omaha Beach. Many large trees gave shade and cover. *AAF photo*

Normandy A-13

A-13 was a beautiful field consisting of two long, pierced-steel-plank (PSP) runways cut out of the tall trees and interlocking hedgerows within sight of the barrage balloons protecting the British Gold Beach nearby. Noteworthy were the oddly sculpted tall trees in the area, which had been trimmed before the war to look somewhat like palm trees. With the arrival of the flight echelon (the aircraft), mostly by July 31, the green foliage became yellow from dust.

Under control of the 70th Wing and IX TAC during the first two weeks of August, the group ran column cover for the armored units fanning out below St. Lô toward Carentan and Avranches. They also flew close-support missions against armor and gun positions, as well as armed reconnaissance missions nearly to the Seine. The pilots learned to use large-scale maps to identify targets as they worked with controllers operating with the ground units.

Especially notable features of life at A-13 were the trips to the front. "Reconnaissance parties" of 406th FG personnel explored the Normandy line from Cane to the sea and actually entered Granville, Carentan, Avranches, and St. James before Allied troops. The results included acquisition of some liberated transportation and equipment, as well as many tall tales about narrow escapes from the enemy.

After the 406th spent two weeks in the eastern part of the beachhead, the Allied armies broke into the Brest Peninsula, and Third Army was committed. The group was reassigned to its original higher headquarters, the 303rd Fighter Wing and XIX TAC. This necessitated a move away from the eastern part of the battle area in order to be near the fight in the west. The air echelon packed up and drove to temporary airfield A-20 at Lessay. There they found the field almost unusable due to enemy demolition. After the air echelon had hustled to get set up, movement orders for the flight and ground echelons to Lessay were canceled.

Two days later, the two separated parts of the group were ordered to move simultaneously to A-14, near Cretteville. The next day was a busy one! With the help of twenty quartermaster trucks, the move was made. Working late into the night created sufficient organization to fly a mission the next day, but it was four or five days before all the sections were functioning and everyone had a place to eat and sleep.

Temporary Airfield A-36. Located near Le Mans. Sundays saw large crowds of local French visitors. *Courtesy of Pima Air & Space Museum*

Normandy A-14

The setting at A-14 was idyllic. The *406th Occupier* records this: Combat Ops established itself under a high canopy of trees behind a chateau close by the field with the three Squadron operations nearby immediately across a dry moat which enclosed the entire surroundings. All officers in the Group were billeted in the chateau or in the courtyard in front and the mess set up in adjoining servant's quarters. There was good weather, relief from the dust, and adequate space in the chateau for a rather elaborate Officer's club and bar."

Missions in these days were characteristic of airpower in its most flexible and versatile form. As the breakout phase continued into the exploitation stage, the Group would fly a fighter sweep into Brest, dive bomb the encircled garrison at St. Malo, support Third Army armor driving for Le Mans, and fly armed recce to the Seine on successive missions. Those were the days of the Falaise pocket and disorderly retreat when fat targets were plentiful and claims good. Too the German Air Force made one of its sporadic attempts to put up a fight at this point.

From the few fields remaining to them in the Dreux and Paris area they attempted to protect the retreat across the Seine and interfere with our bridgehead being established at Mantes-Gassicourt. The result was frequent sightings and some encounters, the most important of which was on August 19.

The mission that day was flown to destroy barges on the Seine River. The 513th FS had made their attacks, destroying five barges and damaging others. Gas and ammunition were running low as they began heading for home. Just 10 miles northwest of Paris, the flight of the 513th DO (director of operations), Maj. Henry Shurlds, was bounced by a series of two, four, six, and finally three more Bf 109s. The Germans attacked in waves, hoping to introduce more planes into the fight unseen so they could get easy shots. Lt. Raymond Stewart's plane was hit and on fire. He jettisoned the canopy and prepared to bail out. Suddenly the fire went out, so he stayed with the aircraft. Maj. Shurlds was also hit and his Thunderbolt exploded; no parachute. Another 513th pilot, Lt. Robert O'Neill, disappeared during the fight and was reported missing at the end of the mission.

Meanwhile, the 512th was finishing their attacks on the barges and heard the radio calls of the 513th: "Split-S, you have one on your tail!" "They got Shurlds. He blew up!" They looked toward the 513th and saw a swarm of fighter planes in a swirling fur ball. Capt. Jesse Underwood made a beeline for the fight, with 1Lt. William Anderson Jr. and Capt. Jack Bronson close behind him. They saw approximately thirty Bf 109s attacking the 513th. Then a blue-nosed Thunderbolt from the 514th passed them with six 109s on his tail. Underwood engaged, setting the first two 109s on fire. The 109s lost interest in the 514th P-47.

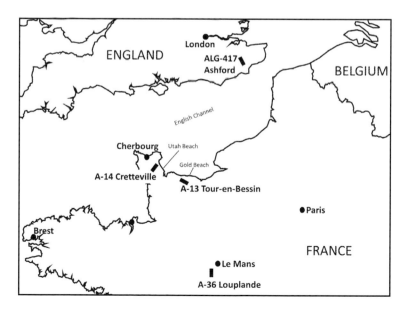

Map of 406th FG bases in England and Normandy

These 512th FS aircraft are taking off from Normandy. *Courtesy of Pima Air and Space Museum*

Just then, someone called, "Look out, Bronson!" on the radio. At the same moment, Jack Bronson heard the chatter of 20 mm cannon over his shoulder. He turned hard. The German overshot and kept going. Bronson saw another 109 burning and took a shot at it. Then he noticed that the cockpit was empty. The German pilot had already bailed out! Bronson looked down and saw three tan German parachutes floating down. He didn't see 1Lt. John Brown's white parachute also in the air. Brown was a newly arrived replacement pilot on his first combat mission, flying 1Lt. Jack Yarger's newly acquired bubbletop P-47D-27RE 42-28436 L3-I. He was hit, caught fire, and bailed out. Yarger never got to fly his new plane in combat!

The German fighters disappeared as quickly as they had materialized, all but two 109s that Underwood, Anderson, and Bronson were chasing down the Seine toward Paris at fairly low altitude. Anderson got a good deflection shot on one of the 109s. The German's wing came off and went flying by Bronson. Underwood was taking shots at the other 109, forcing him to turn. This allowed Bronson to catch up. He took a shot at the 109 with almost no deflection and got strikes all over the German's cockpit. The 109 rolled over and crashed into a building.

It seemed all of Paris was shooting at the three 512th Thunderbolts. Underwood's plane was hit. It was smoking and losing oil, losing power. The three flew over Versailles at very low altitude, headed southwest. Anderson climbed to try to get radio contact and a DF steer to the newly opened Allied airfield at Angiers. Bronson stayed with Underwood. They overflew American Sherman tanks, then found themselves over German troops in the Falaise Gap. Underwood's engine seized, and he bailed out. He hit the trees before ever opening his parachute. Bronson circled over him and saw him lying on the ground, with German soldiers approaching him. Bronson figured there was nothing more he could do, and so he headed back to A-14.

Meanwhile, two more Bf 109s were claimed by the 513th, but neither one was shot down. One hit a tree while chasing Lt. Stewart in his damaged but still-flying Thunderbolt. The other plunged into the Seine while trying to get a shot at Lt. Roddey Ellis.

Capt. Underwood came to his senses, with someone calling to him in thickly accented English: "Stand up!" He realized that he could. He wasn't injured other than a few bruises! Although he had not deployed his parachute, the trees had broken his fall. The Germans were in full retreat. The soldiers who captured him took him to a field hospital, but he easily slipped away. He made his way back to American lines and then back to the 406th at A-14.

Lt. O'Neill also returned to the group on September 11, 1944, with an interesting story of his evasion. He lived for eleven days with a French family and during that time succeeded in capturing two German soldiers! Lt. O'Neill also claimed one enemy plane destroyed during the aerial battle.

The 406th claimed six destroyed and three damaged that day for the loss of Maj. Henry Shurlds. The other three 406th pilots who went down made it back to the unit. 1Lt. John Brown was badly burned, however. He was captured, patched up by a French doctor, then allowed to escape.

Normandy A-36

As the rapidly moving front continued on beyond the Seine, toward the Meuse, it was evident that the 406th would be moving again. By September 1, the group was on its way to the next spot, A-36, near Le Mans. The air echelon moved into the site during the first few days of September, before construction was completed. They were followed by the flight and ground echelons nearly a week later. The group came under the control of the 100th Fighter Wing and was immediately put to work. Missions included supporting the 79th Infantry Division and 2nd French Armored Division, sweeping through eastern France, and, to the west, aiding the US VIII Corps in their assault on the fortress of Brest.

The group mastered living under field conditions at A-36. Though covered completely in tents, the areas were nicely arranged and the weather was warm. The part of France surrounding Le Mans had suffered little destruction from the war because the Germans had pulled out so quickly. It was a rich rural area, very inviting to personnel of the group. They ventured out among the natives more than ever before. Recently liberated Paris was also the object of many visits, and there was a dinner party at nearby Lafleche nearly every evening. The locals also came out to A-36 to see airpower in action. Sundays in particular saw huge crowds of civilian spectators visiting the field.

Operations in September 1944 started off with an impromptu but very successful attack on Metz Airdrome by the 514th FS. While flying armed reconnaissance above broken clouds, 1Lt. Hilton Lewis spotted many enemy planes dispersed around the airfield. Maj. George Ruddell led the squadron in for a devastating strafing attack. They claimed twelve aircraft destroyed on the ground and dozens damaged.

Days later, the US 7th Army began to drive north out of southern France, forcing the enemy to make for the Belfort Gap. Planes of the group ranged to the east on armed reconnaissance missions, making particularly effective attacks in the vicinity of Dijon. When the final assault on Brest began, the 406th dive-bombed dug-in positions immediately in front of the advancing infantry. On one mission the 513th FS attacked enemy ships in Brest harbor with bombs and rockets. Capt. Raymond Walsh sank a German warship with a salvo of rockets! At this same time, XIX TAC had been given the task of protecting with airpower the right flank of Gen. Patton's 3rd Army as it raced across France. The 406th played a major part in the successful accomplishment of that tasking.

Courtesy of Pima Air and Space Museum

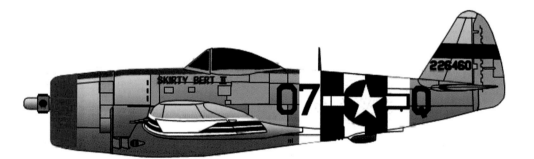

It is not absolutely certain that 42-26460 had the name "SKIRTY BERT II" painted on it. But it is clear that the aircraft was assigned to Maj. Kelly and that one of the aircraft assigned to him at about that time was named "SKIRTY BERT II." Unfortunately, in the photo that shows the name, the serial number is hidden by a Cletrac.

Photo from gun camera film of 514th FS strike on Metz airfield. *Courtesy of Pima Air and Space Museum*

Photo from gun camera film of 513th FS strike on Brest harbor. *Courtesy of Pima Air and Space Museum*

These 512th FS aircraft are parked at airfields in Normandy. *All photos courtesy of Pima Air and Space Museum*

This P-47 apparently caught fire and burned up after landing. Trees identify the airfield as A-13.

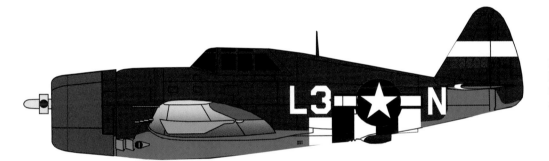

P-47D-5RE 42-8508, inherited from the 353rd FG, had obviously been damaged and repaired. Both wings were bare metal except for an olive-drab-and-gray left aileron.

These 406th FG aircraft are parked at an airfield in Normandy.

Maj. Richard Graves of the 513th FS. He was KIA due to flak on February 23, 1945. Note the bare-metal right wing on an olive-drab-and-gray Thunderbolt.

The assigned pilot for this P-47D-27RE was 1Lt. John B. Yarger, but he never flew it in combat. The plane was shot down by Bf 109 on its first combat sortie on August 19. The pilot that day was 1Lt. John C. Brown, a "new guy."

512th FS aircraft at an airfield in Normandy. *Courtesy of Pima Air and Space Museum*

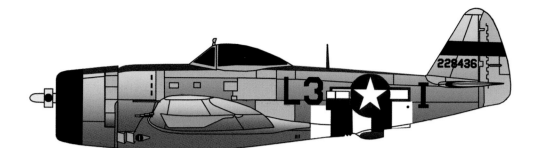

A P-47 providing column cover. *AAF photo*

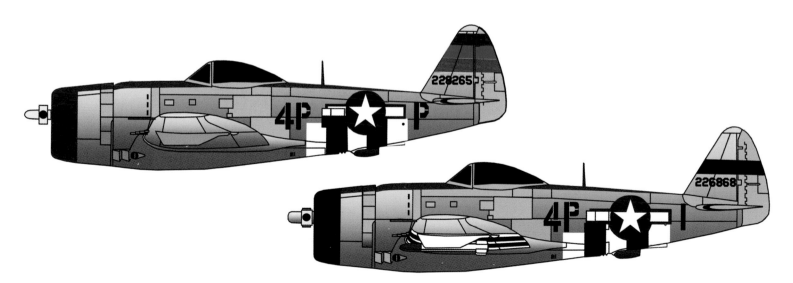

This P-47D-27RE made a belly landing and burned September 13, 1944, near Dompaire, France. The pilot, Wendell D. Brady, returned to the 513th FS.

Newly received 406th FG P-47 at an airfield in Normandy. ID codes have not yet been painted on. *All photos courtesy of Pima Air and Space Museum*

This 512th FS aircraft is taking off from an airfield in Normandy.

406th FG P-47 after forced landing in Normandy. Rugged Thunderbolt protected its pilot.

CHAPTER 6
Belfort Gap

The *406th Occupier* records, "On September 7, at 1400 hours in the afternoon TAC pilots of the Command spotted a large column of enemy vehicles, horse[-]drawn carts, ammunition carriers and personnel between Chateaureux and Issoudun, France. Taking off as soon as possible, the Group located the road clogged with all kinds of enemy transport and attacked the column up and down its full length until their ammunition and load were expended, leaving over 300 vehicles destroyed and the road strewn with personnel and wreckage. Returning to base and reloading as fast as possible, the Group returned to the scene of the previous attack and again worked it over, adding another 200 claims to the total."

Immediately following the terrible destruction from the air, German general Eric Elster agreed to surrender his 20,000 troops on condition that the air attacks would stop. The surrender was accomplished to Maj. Gen. Robert C. Macon, commander of the 83rd Infantry Division, but with Maj. Gen. O. P. Weyland, commander of XIX TAC, participating in the ceremony. For this decisive action the 406th FG was awarded a Presidential Unit Citation.

During September 1944, 3rd Army reached the Moselle and the group began interdiction of Alsace-Lorraine. The 406th attacked marshaling yards at Saarbruken, Zabern, Saarburg, and other key rail centers. These targets were soon heavily defended, and Thunderbolts frequently returned from missions with battle damage. Others did not return. The 512th FS alone lost seven pilots in September. Their commander, Maj. John Locke, was also shot down, for the second time in thirty days, but made it safely back to the squadron.

Gun camera film from 513th FS pilot Lt. Willie Whitman documents the deadly task of strafing German motorized transports. That's Capt. Raymond Walsh flying into the fireball and flying debris. He survived. The action recorded in these photos occurred on August 10, 1944. Less than a month later, thirty-six P-47s from the 406th, twelve from each squadron, performed similar attacks on a massive German column attempting to escape from France through the Belfort Gap. The action won a Presidential Unit Citation.

Both photos this page courtesy of Pima Air and Space Museum

CHAPTER 7
Mourmelon-le-Grand

P-47s from the 513th FS ready for takeoff at Mourmelon-le-Grand

Airfield A-80, Chalons-sur-Marne, France September 23, 1944– February 2, 1945

The group's next operating location, airfield A-80 at Mourmelon-le-Grand, was their first base east of the Seine, near the Marne River between Chalons-sur-Marne and Reims. The move began on September 20 and was completed on the twenty-third. Mourmelon was an old and well-established military base dating from before the Franco-Prussian War. It had been the site for an artillery unit of the German army, and its grass airfield had served the Luftwaffe. Army engineers had upgraded the runway surface with Hessian matting.

The buildings were in a poor state of repair, but they were buildings—brick buildings! The hope of not having to spend the winter in tents must have warmed the hearts of everyone. The group established itself in the portion of the base nearest the air strip. The facilities were quite comfortable. There was even an officer's club with a swimming pool, though that eventually froze over. The 512th FS officers had some fun getting the squadron mascot, English bulldog "Andy," out on the ice! Officers and upper enlisted grades were housed in cottages sleeping three to eight, some of which had been originally built as stables for Napoleon's cavalry. The lower enlisted grades were housed in larger brick buildings. All buildings featured stoves that could burn wood or coal and stave off the cold.

The end of September and most of the month of October were devoted to interdiction of the area between the Saar and the Moselle. The 406th constantly policed the rails for movement and cut rail lines as needed to stop that movement. The group also attacked many marshaling yards in the region. During one of these antirail attacks near Haguenau on October 22, Capt. Noah Lewin-Epstein of the 514th FS, flying Capt. J. C. Van Bloom's "Bloom's Tomb VI," hit a steel post and tore off 4.7 feet of the plane's left wing. He returned to A-80 for a very hot landing with no airspeed indication!

The L3-L of 512th FS commander John L. Locke. In this aircraft, Locke was shot down for the second time in thirty days on September 20, 1944. He returned to the squadron the same day.

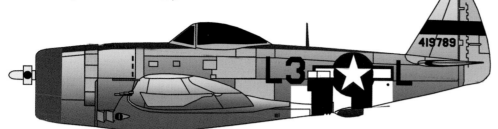

Maj. John L. Locke. *Courtesy of Pima Air and Space Museum*

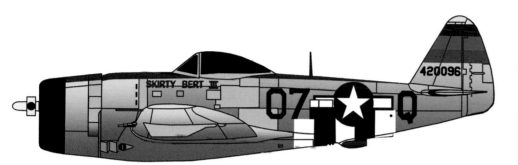

514th FS commander Converse B. Kelly's 07-Q "SKIRTY BERT III." Lost due to flak on November 19, 1944, near Wellingen, Germany. The pilot was Lt. Richard Armstrong. Bailed out but KIA.

Maj. Converse B. Kelly. *Courtesy of Pima Air and Space Museum*

A-80 in September 1944. C-47s brought supplies not only to the 406th but also, starting in late November 1944, to the 101st Airborne Division, which moved to Mourmelon-le-Grand to rest and refit. *Courtesy of Pima Air and Space Museum*

The grassy parking areas were soon churned into mud. 512th FS P-47 and visiting P-38 in the mud at A-80 with badly damaged flightline buildings in the background.

The 406th also provided close air support to units of 3rd US Army during October. A notable mission of this type occurred on the seventh. Directed by a ground controller, the 513th and 514th Squadrons made a fragmentation bomb attack on a heavily defended patch of woods south of Nomeny. Afterward, ground forces moved in and captured over 2,500 shocked and bewildered German soldiers who were wandering around aimlessly among the bodies of many, many more who had been killed.

Interdiction and bridge-busting attacks continued in November, though worsening weather often interfered. Then, on November 8, 1944, XX Corps started its attack on the fortress of Metz. The 406th flew many close support missions for this bitter fighting and also supported the XII Corps in its drive to the Saar River. This period saw extensive use of the new napalm bombs.

The weather worsened as November progressed into December. Activity on the ground and in the air decreased. It became apparent that the war would not be over by Christmas. Dark skies and bitter cold slowed the pace of operations to almost caretaker status. With little action requiring their attention, the commanders of the group and all three squadrons, along with many of the most experienced pilots, were sent to the States for thirty days' Christmas leave.

Courtesy of Pima Air and Space Museum

This 514th FS P-47 came to grief in the mud at A-80.

2Lt. William Cunningham looks over a muddy parking area at A-80 in November 1944. Aircraft in the background, L3-R, 42-28918, was destroyed in an unfortunate accident a few days later. *Courtesy of Cunningham family*

Tragedy

On December 2, 1944, 1Lt. Arner M. Douglas, in P-47D-28RE 44-19712 L3-K, was leading a four-ship flight, attempting to land at airfield A-82 in bad weather and receiving radar vectors from a tactical radar site, call sign Ripsaw. Three of the four Thunderbolts hit high terrain and were destroyed. The pilot of the fourth, 2Lt. Thomas Downey, just missed the hill. He landed, badly shaken.

2Lt. Thomas Armstrong was leading the other element of the flight in 42-29179 L3-N, with Downey on his right wing. He had moved slightly away from Douglas when they hit. That move may have saved Downey.

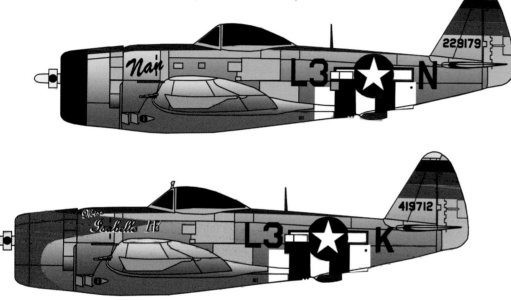

42-29179 at A-80. *Courtesy of Pima Air and Space Museum*

"Miss Isabelle IV" was named for Douglas's wife.

44-19712 in Normandy, before it received squadron markings and name. *Courtesy of Pima Air and Space Museum*

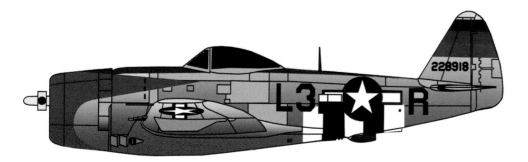

Lt. Thomas Harkinson was flying on Douglas's left wing in 42-28918 when they hit.

1Lt. Arner M. Douglas *Courtesy of Pima Air and Space Museum*

CHAPTER 8

Mud!

2Lt. William Cunningham and 1Lt. Walker Diamanti with 42-26860 in the mud at A-80. *Both photos courtesy of Cunningham family*

If there was a constant that described all of the 406th's airfields throughout the war, it was the ever-present mud. Capt. Carl Matthews, writer of the 512th Fighter Squadron's official history, described ALG 417 at Ashford as "throbbing with mud." Except for a relatively dry August and September in Normandy, when dust took over as the main irritant, mud was always causing trouble. The mud bogged down vehicles, pulled off boots, fowled landing gear, and even caused P-47s to nose over. The bottoms of the planes were coated with mud, and the bombs and external fuel tanks were smeared with it. Every tire and boot was caked with mud.

At A-36 the softness of the mud under the tar paper and metal mats allowed the matting to balloon up ahead of P-47s on takeoff. This happened to 2Lt. Thomas Downey on September 13, 1944, preventing him from getting airborne until almost the end of the runway. His partially retracted landing gear hit stumps at the end of the runway, and the plane cartwheeled. His next recollection was hanging upside down by his safety harness in what remained of the P-47's fuselage as the 512th FS flight surgeon, Doc Edgar Knowlton, cut him free and dragged him away from the wreckage. Downey would later become the sole survivor of the December 2 tragedy.

But nowhere was the mud quite as bad as at Mourmelon-le-Grand. September's grassy parking areas had been torn and beaten by heavy use, so that very little grass remained. The rich French soil mixed with the frequent autumn rains to create an endless gooey mess that nothing could escape. The runway with its Hessian matting was slightly better, but still only barely usable.

A temporary reprieve came with freezing weather. The mud became like concrete at night, only partly thawing in the daytime. Frozen ruts jarred the men as their vehicles bounced over them. On the coldest days in December and January, snow came and stayed, mercifully hiding the mud for a while. But soon slightly warmer weather returned and the snow departed. Constant freezing and thawing made A-80 a quagmire.

In the end, the mud won. By the middle of January, one good final thaw made A-80 inoperable. The 406th moved their planes to Y-79, near Reims, some 8 miles north, and operated them from there. This lasted only a few days. A few more days in the mud at Metz, then on to temporary airfield Y-29 at Asch, Belgium . . . and miles of mud!

Mud was everywhere at A-80. *Courtesy of Pima Air and Space Museum*

A P-47 stuck in the mud at A-80. Note bare metal vertical stabilizer on OD and gray razorback Thunderbolt. *Courtesy of Pima Air and Space Museum*

2Lt. William Cunningham with 42-26860 in the mud at A-80. *Courtesy of Cunningham family*

The 406th got a respite from the mud when they first moved to the Continent. The dry weather of August and early September 1944 turned the mud into thick, choking dust. Pilots had to space out their takeoffs to avoid having the dust from the previous plane obscure their view of the runway during takeoff roll! This lasted until rain came and the dust turned back into mud. It was hard to know which one to hope for!

Thunderbolts taking off in thick dust. *AAF*

Mud at Y-29. All photo courtesy of Pima Air and Space Museum

CHAPTER 9
Snow

The coldest winter in memory turned a barren landscape at A-80 into an even-bleaker picture. Fortunately, personnel were housed in brick buildings with stoves for heat. Pyramid tents were for the flight line only.

Snow at A-80.

All photos courtesy of Pima Air and Space Museum

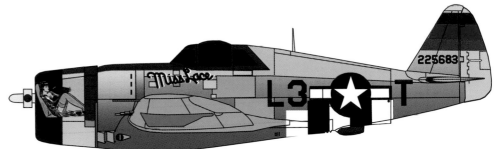

Lt. Donal (not Donald!) Whicker's popular and long-lived mount apparently came to the 512th already adorned with the "Miss Lace" name and artwork inspired by Milt Caniff's sexy cartoon character. These markings were also on the plane when it served with the 48th Fighter Group. Note the rare Malcolm Hood canopy modification for improved visibility.

Both photos this page courtesy of Pima Air and Space Museum

Nose blazes in squadron colors adorned many of the group's P-47s during December 1944.

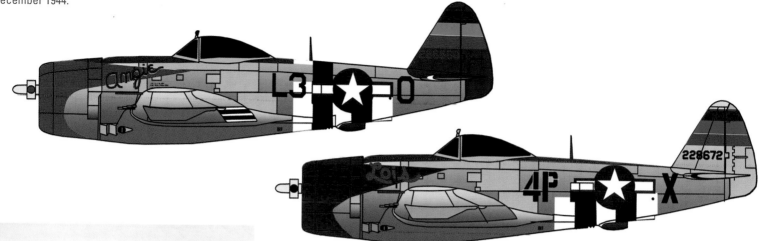

The group markings of three stripes on the tail in the three squadron colors were even more common . . .

Snow at A-80. *Courtesy of Pima Air and Space Museum*

Courtesy of Linda Martin

. . . but many black noses still remained.

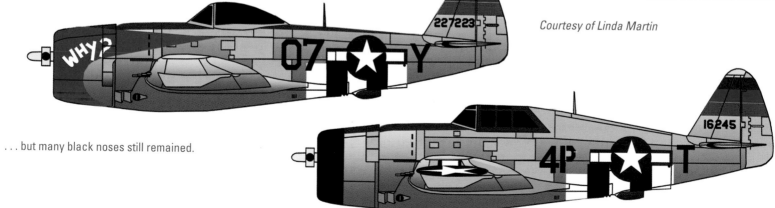

One of the few P-47C Thunderbolts handed down to the 406th FG from the 8th AF, 41-6245 was still flying with the 513th FS in December 1944.

Enlisted quarters in two-story brick buildings at Mourmelan-le-Grand and officer quarters in cottages made operating in the snow and bitter cold just a little more bearable than it would have been if living in tents. *AAF*

Heater carts facilitated cold-weather maintenance. Note bare metal cowling and cowl flaps on olive drag and gray Thunderbolt. C-47 in background is missing its rudder. *Courtesy of Pima Air and Space Museum*

Flexible hose attached to heater cart carried hot air to warm hands and hardware at the point where maintenance work was being done. *Courtesy of Pima Air and Space Museum*

CHAPTER 10
The Bulge

Returning from mission to Bastogne. *Courtesy of Pima Air and Space Museum*

Beginning in November 1944, elements of the 101st Airborne Division began arriving at Mourmelon-le-Grand to rest and refit. A close relationship soon grew up between the two organizations, as they shared USO shows, C-47s bringing supplies to the 101st used the 406th's airstrip, and paratroopers traded war souvenirs for wine and champagne that 406th officers could obtain from nearby Reims and Epernay. Some men, such as Jack Bronson of the 406th, found old schoolmates among the Screaming Eagles, leading to happy reunions.

On the night of December 17, an officer of the 101st came to the 406th Combat Ops center and asked to use the phone to recall some of his troops. By morning there was news of the German counteroffensive in the Ardennes, and the 101st was aboard trucks on its way to Bastogne. They were soon surrounded in that crucial junction town.

There followed five days of impenetrable fog in which no flying was possible. Frequent reports came in indicating the seriousness of the situation. Guard protection of the base was doubled. Ground crews worked day and night getting all available aircraft ready to go when the weather permitted. Pilots hung around the ready rooms, eager for the order to launch. On the morning of December 23, 1944, the skies cleared. At first light the Thunderbolts of the 406th were off to save their friends at Bastogne.

For five successive days from sunup to sunset, the group provided constant air support over Bastogne, making attack after attack within a 10-mile radius of the town. The 406th flew over 519 sorties during those hectic days. They faced extreme difficulties caused by the fluid front lines, German use of American equipment, frequent appearance of the Luftwaffe, and the most intense light flak ever encountered. But the group pressed home their attacks, causing carnage among the enemy that was staggering, blunting the German drive and relieving the 101st. On three successive mornings, planes from the group arrived over Bastogne just as the Germans were starting a major offensive that without intervention from the air would have overrun the town.

The 406th lost ten pilots in those days. One of these, 1Lt. William H. Nellis of the 513th FS, was immortalized in 1950 when Nellis AFB, near his hometown of Las Vegas, Nevada, was named after him. Nellis is famous as the home of USAF Fighter Weapons School and the Red Flag exercises.

Of the sixty-plus aircraft assigned to the 406th in December 1944, over forty suffered battle damage. On the morning of December 28, after five days of intense activity, the entire 406th FG had only twelve serviceable planes. Those five days were critical, but the task of beating the enemy back into the Siegfried Line lasted well into January. The group underwent constant air and ground alerts every night, then by day flew mission after mission. The 406th's crucial part in the Battle of the Bulge and direct support of the beleaguered 101st Airborne garrison at Bastogne during those pivotal days won them their second Presidential Unit Citation.

Ready for takeoff for Bastogne

Map of 406th FG bases in eastern France and Belgium

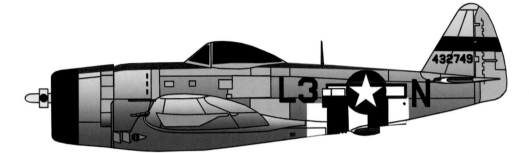

P-47D-30RA 44-32749 apparently replaced 42-29719 as L3-N after the latter crashed on December 2, 1944. The frenetic pace of operations at the end of 1944 did not allow time to paint on squadron and group markings.

On January 1, 1945, 2Lt. Raymond R. Francis, flying aircraft "I," had his wing damaged by a falling bomb near Bastogne. He was forced to land at A-82.

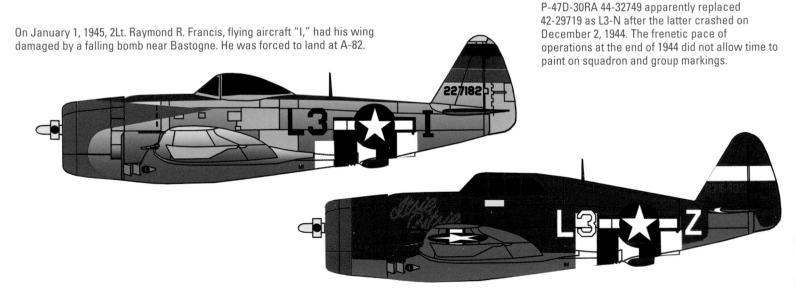

This aircraft and pilot 2Lt. Leo J. Didas were lost due to flak near Bastogne on January 2, 1945.

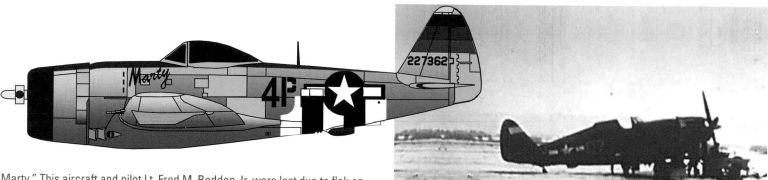

"Marty." This aircraft and pilot Lt. Fred M. Bodden Jr. were lost due to flak on December 25, 1944, near Salle/Bertogne, Belgium.

Snow at A-80. *Photo courtesy of Pima Air and Space Museum*

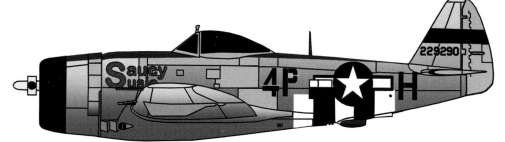

"Saucy Susie." Seen in the snow without rocket stubs, P-47D-28RA 42-29290 4P-H was probably another replacement that arrived during those busy days. The rocket stubs and squadron colors would be added when time permitted. The assigned pilot was Lt. Arden A. Hitch.

Snow at A-80. *Photo courtesy of Pima Air and Space Museum*

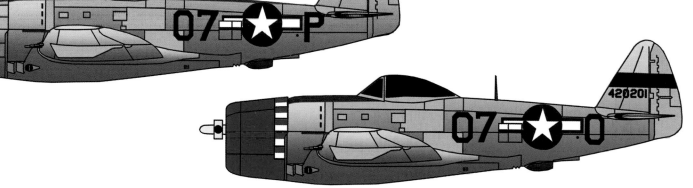

Lt. Bob Gilbert's 07-O "Miss Jean" had nose art that is not discernible in the photo and so is not shown.

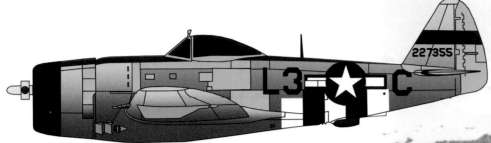

Aircraft hit by flak near Bastogne and returned to A-80 for belly landing

Belly landing at A-80. *Courtesy of Pima Air and Space Museum*

Note that the commanders of the group and all three squadrons, along with many of the most-experienced pilots, had left in early December for thirty days' leave in the States. So, during the Battle of the Bulge, the 406th FG was commanded by Lt. Col. Leslie R. Bratton, and the 512th FS was commanded by Capt. Jack Bronson. Bronson pinned on major on December 30! Maj. Richard D. Graves led the 513th while Maj. Gordon W. Fowler was on leave, and Maj. George I. Ruddell commanded the 514th while Maj. Kelly was gone.

Brig. Gen. Anthony C. McAuliffe, who commanded the 101st Airborne Division at Bastogne, said to the men of the 406th, "I never knew until now that fighter-bombers could do so much. If it had not been for your splendid air support, we should never have been able to hold out." Gen. McAuliffe is better known for his reply to the Germans when they demanded the surrender of Bastogne. He said, "Nuts!"

Newly pinned-on Maj. Jack Bronson. *Courtesy of Pima Air and Space Museum*

406th FG Thunderbolt drops napalm on the snowy landscape. *Courtesy of Pima Air and Space Museum*

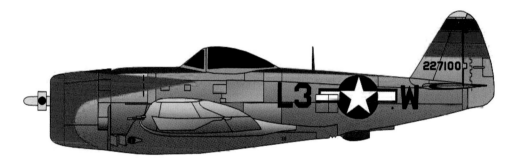

This aircraft was hit by flak on January 15, 1945. Pilot Elton F. Bacon bailed out over friendly territory, returned to the squadron.

Tracked vehicle burning in the snow. *Courtesy of Pima Air and Space Museum*

CHAPTER 11
Repairs

Horizontal tail replaced in field with salvaged part. *All photos this page courtesy of Pima Air and Space Museum*

On December 28, 1944, after five days of constant fighting around Bastogne, the entire 406th FG had only twelve flyable P-47s.

The tireless work by the ground crews to keep the group in the air is showcased by the three-photo sequence showing the bare-metal P-47 44-32749 L3-N getting a replacement olive-drab horizontal stabilizer salvaged from an older P-47. The harsh conditions are apparent. This incident probably occurred at A-80 during the Battle of the Bulge. Later photos show that the olive-drab stabilizer was still on the aircraft after the end of the war. Note the use of bombs for a workstand!

Damage that would require a replacement horizontal stabilizer. Pilot is Lt. Francis E. Lewis of the 514th FS. Plane was hit by flak while strafing and the left wing was also damaged. When hit, the plane rolled inverted, but Lewis managed to level off inverted and avoid hitting the ground. He righted the aircraft and returned to A-80 for a belly landing. Before the photo was taken, the aircraft had been raised by a crane and the gear extended.

512th FS aircraft parked at Y-29, including 43-28887 with OD rudder and right elevator. *All photos courtesy of Pima Air and Space Museum*

The 406th Fighter Group boneyard, source of many replacement parts.

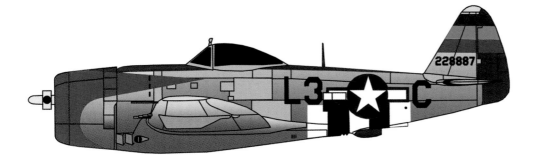

Contrasting rudder color was not a group or squadron marking but rather the result of replacing damaged surfaces with ones cannibalized from other aircraft.

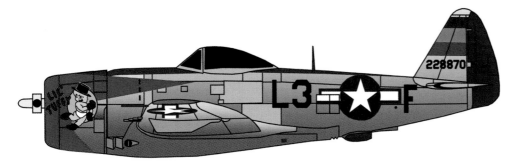

P-47 42-28870 "Li'l Tuffy" was assigned to Lt. Harold Cox, who scored two air-to-air kills in February 1945.

Thunderbolts frequently returned from missions with tail sections severely damaged by flak. If the enemy gunners found their mark further forward on the aircraft, those planes often did not return.

CHAPTER 12
Metz

Wrecked aircraft at Y-34. *Photo courtesy of Pima Air and Space Museum*

Temporary Airfield Y-34, Metz, France
February 2–6, 1945

The move to airfield Y-34, near Metz, France, had been planned for several weeks but was delayed by the Battle of the Bulge. Finally, on January 31, 1945, the air echelon proceeded to Y-34. Despite a shortage of transportation and roads covered with snow and ice, most of the unit was successfully moved to Metz by February 3.

Moving to Metz was ironic, in that while it was used by the Germans, the 406th had on at least one occasion strafed the field with good effect, destroying many aircraft. The hulks of those planes still remained on the field. Then, on January 1, 1945, as part of Operation Bodenplatte, the German Luftwaffe bombed and strafed the field, then used by the Americans, destroying several P-47s of the 365th FG. Those hulks also littered the area. The flight-line buildings had been well worked over by both air forces, so they were in bad shape. Even trees and bushes showed the signs of many air attacks.

From the *406th Occupier*: "After running one mission from the new field on the 4th in the afternoon . . . Lt. Col. Leslie R. Bratton, the acting group commander, called his staff together and in hushed tones informed them that we had been transferred to XXIX TAC far to the north and would proceed to Y-29 in Asch, Belgium[,] so as to be operational from that field on the 7th of February. All agreed that it could not be done but that we would have to try. An advanced party of sorts left immediately for the new site and through the help of an Air Force fleet of trucks and C-47 transports, the move was begun the next day."

At 0700 on February 6, the air echelon was loaded on trucks and ready to go. At 1630 that day, the convoy arrived at Y-29 without mishap. The drive took them through Bastogne and Houffalise, where they witnessed the aftermath of the Battle of the Bulge. Intensive effort in the next two days got the organization ready to operate from the new base. On February 8, the move was completed when the flight echelon flew in the unit's P-47s. Some of these launched from A-34, performed a mission, and then landed at Y-29.

Wrecked and burned-out buildings at Y-34. *AAF*

Wrecked German planes at Y-34 that had been bulldozed aside to clear the field for operations. *AAF*

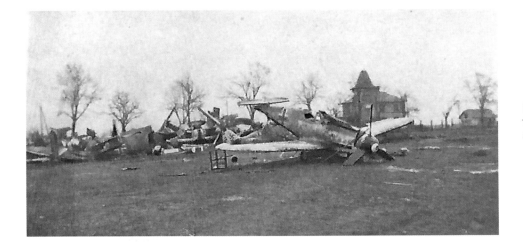

More wrecked German planes still littered the parking areas at Y-34. Even the trees showed scars of multiple air attacks. *AAF*

CHAPTER 13
Asch

Temporary Airfield Y-29, Asch, Belgium
February 6–April 15, 1945

Y-29 was somewhat famous for a New Year's Day air attack, part of the Luftwaffe Operation Bodenplatte, that turned into a slaughter of the attacking Germans. The 366th FG, which had gotten twelve kills flying from Y-29 on January 1, 1945, was still stationed at the field. They shared the single runway at Y-29 with the 406th.

Aircraft markings were in transition when the group moved to Asch. The intense action in December and January, the large influx of replacement aircraft, and the superhuman efforts by ground crews to repair and piece together planes to keep them in the fight, all of which occurred just before two moves, ensured that there was no "typical" set of markings for the group's P-47s in February 1945. In this photo, taken at Y-29, markings range from L3-E "Lilly Gay," with no squadron or group markings at all other than white L3s, to L3-L, with full nose blaze and tail stripes. In between is a very nonstandard razorback with olive-drab upper half and bare-metal lower half, plus a unique nose blaze and no aircraft ID letter!

512th FS aircraft preparing to taxi at Y-29. *Courtesy of Pima Air and Space Museum*

"Wee Winnie," 42-26661, was assigned to 1Lt. Donal Whicker, who had three kills by this date. 2Lt. William Cunningham bailed out of this aircraft on March 14, 1945, and became a POW.

Engine change alfresco. *Courtesy of Pima Air and Space Museum*

P-47 42-75527 "Lilly Gay" had obviously been damaged and repaired several times by February 1945.

512th FS P-47 44-21086 L3-A landing at Y-29. *Photo from AAF film crew via US National Archives*

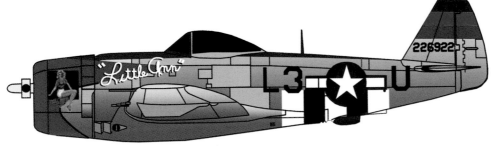

All photos courtesy of Pima Air and Space Museum

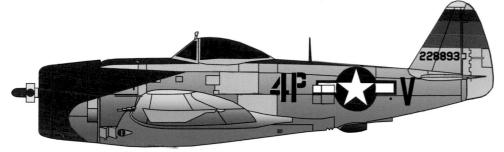

By this date the 513th had begun painting propeller hubs in the squadron color.

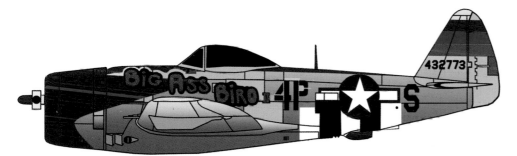

"Big Ass Bird II," but there were at least two previous P-47s so named. The pilot was 1Lt. Howard M. Park. Park had one air-to-air kill by this date and would get one more on March 1, 1945.

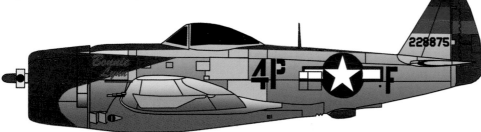

P-47D-28-RA 42-28875 4P-F "Bonnie Lynn" was shot down by flak on April 12, 1945. The pilot, John A. Bolle, was KIA.

Sign post in a nearby village: "Asch 6 km"

1Lt. Howard M. Park looking mean in 44-32773.

"My Baby." Pilot: Lt. J. G. Barber. The name was added and under-fuselage invasion stripes were removed while at Y-29.

514th FS P-47 44-20428 07-I landing at Y-29. *Photo from AAF film crew via US National Archives*

Some older P-47s received full squadron and group markings while at Y-29.

Photo from AAF film crew via US National Archives

At some point, Col. Kelly's 42-26460 07-Q must have been damaged, replaced, and recycled as 07-A.

Photo from AAF film crew via US National Archives

CHAPTER 14
Operation Clarion

2Lt. Ernie Sprouse and 2Lt. Harold Cox. *Left photo courtesy of Sprouse family*

On February 22, Operation Clarion kicked off. The editor of the *406th Occupier* newspaper wrote that the operation "involved simultaneous use of all available aircraft in the theatre on a tactical strike at strategic rail installations designed to so paralyze the enemy's communications system that he could not effectively defend against the assault on the last remaining Siegfried and Rhine defenses. The Group's mission on this grand show was to escort groups of medium bombers to rail bridges on the northeast fringes of the Ruhr near Gutersloh, where five minutes before reaching the target they would precede the bombers in and dive-bomb. After the subsequent attack by the mediums, in addition to escorting them on withdrawal, we were to strafe rail targets of opportunity."

Complex in concept, it was not too surprising that the mission did not go exactly as planned. The *406th Occupier* continues: "Rendezvous time was changed more than once, but the crowning blow was the fact that after the first squadron and half of the second was airborne, the mediums could not make their assigned time at rendezvous. Because two groups stationed on the same field had to be airborne by squadrons at practically the same time, this hour delay in bomber rendezvous required that the planes which had prematurely taken off had to orbit the field for an hour and a half. The resulting confusion caused the first two squadrons to miss rendezvous and escort a different box of bombers into the assigned target area."

After successfully dive-bombing the target, the two squadrons rendezvoused again with the bombers for withdrawal. A large formation of Bf 109s appeared from nowhere and attempted to attack the B-26s. The 406th FG Thunderbolts surged in to break up the attack. A swirling dogfight ensued, the only such fight with the Luftwaffe by the 9th Air Force on that day.

In the midst of this, Lt. Ernie Sprouse of the 512th was attempting to stick like glue to his element leader, Lt. Harold Cox, as they wove and dodged through the swarm of friendly and enemy fighter planes. Sprouse suddenly found himself at close range behind a 109. Time seemed frozen as he pulled the Jug's nose into perfect alignment and reached to squeeze the trigger on his joystick. The eight .50-caliber machine guns on the Thunderbolt's wings roared and tracers reached out at the German, but Sprouse's plane was so close that only his two inner guns on each wing were getting hits on the enemy. He called, "Get him, Cox!" and pulled hard to get out of the way so his element leader (who was behind him) could shoot. Cox did just that, flaming the Messerschmitt with a long burst from his guns that shredded the enemy plane as Sprouse had cleared his line of fire.

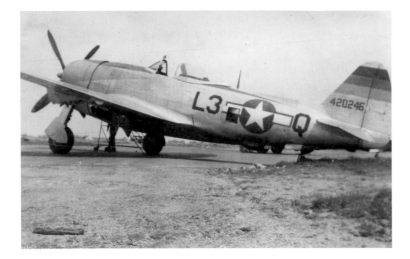

Ernie Sprouse's L3-Q after the dorsal fin was added, but before "Gladys" artwork was painted on cowling. *Photo courtesy of Sprouse family*

Meanwhile, Sprouse's P-47 had entered a "rudder lock." This was a dangerous flight condition made possible when the P-47 design was modified to have a bubble canopy. The reduction in aft fuselage area, which improved visibility to the rear, also reduced the plane's directional stability. So modified, the Thunderbolt could yaw so far that the vertical tail would stall, locking the plane in this extremely yawed condition. Applying rudder to bring it back to streamlined flight would overcorrect, kicking it into an identical stalled-tail yaw in the other direction. The high drag of the extreme sideslip caused Sprouse to lose speed and altitude. The excellent visibility to the rear of his bubble-canopied Thunderbolt allowed him to see a 109 above and behind him in a perfect position to shoot him down. But apparently the wild gyrations of the Thunderbolt made the German decide to go look for an easier target. At some altitude well below 5,000 ft., the thicker air allowed Lt. Sprouse to regain control and fly back to Y-29 on the deck. Republic had developed a fix for this problem, a small dorsal fin that could be added. Modification kits were arriving at the P-47 units, and Sprouse made sure his plane was so modified before he flew it again!

For the day, the 512th claimed five 109s destroyed and seven damaged for the loss of 2Lt. Alfred B. Ford in a brand-new P-47D-

30RE, serial number 44-33048. The 514th did not fare so well, losing three Thunderbolts and pilots while claiming six destroyed and one damaged. Still, considering the bad timing at the beginning of the mission, these two squadrons turned their bad start into an amazing success.

The next day, February 23, 9th US Army launched its drive from the Roer to the Rhine, and the 406th had one of its most successful days. The group, by squadrons, flew both rail interdiction and ground cooperation missions. The 512th FS had a particularly good day, which typifies the success achieved by all three squadrons. 1Lt. Oscar F. Baldwin, who had gotten an air-to-air kill the previous day, led the first mission, taking off with twelve ships at 0815. They started by hitting a railroad bridge and cutting tracks on both sides. 2Lt. Forest B. Claxton, flying as element lead in Red Flight, scored two direct hits on one of the bridge abutments. Shortly thereafter, the squadron spotted a forty-car train loaded with eighty motorized transports, two per car. Yellow and Blue Flights dove in and put six bombs directly on target, with the others near misses. Strafing delivered the coup de grace. The train and its vital cargo were totally destroyed.

Capt. John Akin led the second 512th FS mission off in the late morning of February 23, finding a marshaling yard with 125 cars on sidings. The squadron put all its bombs but two in the target area, cutting the main tracks in three places and destroying sixty-one boxcars. Follow-up strafing silenced twelve pesky flak guns and destroyed a few trucks.

Capt. Fred Marall, 512th DO, who had also flamed a Bf 109 the previous day, led the last mission of the day at 1400. They found another marshaling yard with a live train and fifty cars loaded with tanks, motorized transports, and ammunition. They put all their bombs in the yard, getting six direct hits on the train and cutting the tracks in several places. The ammunition cars exploded with spectacular collateral damage. The locomotive and twenty-five cars were definitely destroyed, along with all the trucks and armor that would never make it to the front. One bomb demolished a building in the yard, and as the Thunderbolts exited the scene, a number of fires were burning. On their way back to Y-29, they found another locomotive with eight cars making a run for it. Strafing stopped the engine and damaged the cars.

The group's outstanding effort that day prompted a written commendation from Brig. Gen. Richard E. Nugent, commander of XXIX TAC. More important, the 406th was fulfilling its assignment to stop all traffic to the front. The appearance of the Luftwaffe on the twenty-second revealed how critical this was to the enemy. The successes on the twenty-third reemphasized how effective fighter-bombers could be at hurting the Germans.

Gun camera film of 406th FG P-47 strafing a train. *Courtesy of Pima Air and Space Museum*

At the same time Claxton was hit, his wingman, 2Lt. Fred Brandt in Blue Four, 44-33010 L3-G, got a brick through his windscreen. The shattered glass cut his face and eyes. He was blind! Other debris hit his propeller, pushing it back until it dented the cowling. Somehow he instinctively pulled out of his dive and managed to keep the plane upright, flying by the "seat of his pants." His eyes were full of blood, especially the left one, which had a shard of glass sticking in it.

The slipstream was howling through the hole where the windscreen had been, battering Brandt's face. He spit on his fingers and tried to rub the blood out of his right eye. He finally got sufficient moisture to rub enough blood out so he could see a little. With this limited vision, he proposed to land at Y-29. He got radar vectors to the airfield, then circled overhead as ground crews prepared for the emergency landing.

The 512th FS continued antirail strikes on February 24, this time to Vohwinkle, a small German town west of Dusseldorf, with Capt. William Anderson Jr. leading twelve P-47s. They found another live train in the marshaling yard there. The Thunderbolts were configured with a 500 lb. bomb on each wing and a bundle of fragmentation bombs on the belly shackle. Following their normal practice, they started off by dive-bombing the yard. Red Flight laid their eggs, then Yellow Flight. Suddenly, as Blue Flight was making their dive-bomb runs, a massive explosion rocked the yard. The explosion threw huge pieces of trains, tracks, and buildings into the air. Lt. Claxton, flying as Blue Three in 44-33318, was hit badly by the explosion. He was still flying, but his main fuselage fuel tank caught fire. It was time to get out!

Capt. Jack Yarger, who was leading Blue Fight, called on the radio: "Claxton, you're on fire. Bail out!" Claxton replied that he wanted to get some altitude first. The clouds were quite low. Claxton disappeared into them climbing, trailing flames and smoke. Yarger chased him. Above the cloud deck, at about 2,000 ft. above the ground, Claxton pushed the nose over and exited the airplane. Yarger saw his chute open above the clouds. The Germans saw him as he descended down below the clouds, and quickly made him a POW after he landed.

Capt. Jack Yarger and Capt. William Anderson. *Courtesy of Pima Air and Space Museum*

Four 512th FS pilots, all from Iowa. *Left to right:* 1Lt. Donal Wicker, 2Lt. Richard Dean, 1Lt. Forest Claxton, and 2Lt. Fred Brandt

A P-47 landing at Y-29 with other planes parked nearby. *Photo from AAF film crew via US National Archives*

The temporary PSP runway at Y-29 was lined with parked airplanes undergoing maintenance, servicing, and loading. When alerted of the emergency landing, ground crews cleared out from around the planes and hurried away from the area to watch from a safe distance. Any crash trucks or other emergency-response vehicles were probably very rudimentary, maybe nonexistent.

2Lt. Brandt made a good landing, then discovered that he had a blown tire and no brakes! With the extra rolling friction of the blown tire, the plane drifted toward the side of the runway, even though Brandt was applying full opposite rudder. This was critical because if the bad wheel ran all the way off the steel planks and into the mud, it would pull his Thunderbolt off the runway and into the parked planes, some probably loaded with bombs and ammunition for the next mission. Somehow, full opposite rudder and pumping the brake on that rudder pedal got the P-47 to turn ever so slightly, and it began drifting back toward the center of the runway.

But at this point the end of the runway was coming up, and the 6-ton Thunderbolt was still moving very fast. If it ran off the end, the wheels would sink into the mud, and the plane would likely flip over its nose and onto its back, pinning Brandt and smothering him in the mud. He slowed down as much as he could, holding the rudder and pumping the brake to stay on the runway, waiting until he had almost reached the end. At the last moment he reversed the rudder pedals, pushing the pedal and brake on the side of the blown tire. This caused the plane to pivot on the wheel with the blown tire, swinging around in what's known as a ground loop. That maneuver dissipated most of the rest of the plane's speed, so the nearly blind pilot could safely steer the plane off the runway, coming to a stop in the mud.

As ground personnel raced up to pull Lt. Brandt from the cockpit, they hesitated, pointing toward the belly of the plane. The fragmentation cluster, wrapped with two metal bands, was still attached to the belly shackle! The sway braces were broken but the cluster hung on, and it didn't detonate.

That was the end of the war for Lt. Brandt. He spent the rest of the time until VE-day in England in a convalescent hospital, waiting for his face and eye to heal. His next flight was on May 15, 1945, just a week after the war ended in Europe.

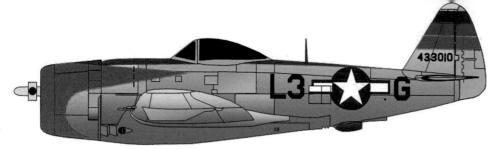

By February 1945, the 406th FG had received many new P-47s. So on February 24, when he was hit and nearly blinded by a railyard explosion, 2Lt. Fred Brandt was not flying his P-47D-27RE 42-26860 L3-O. He was flying a brand new P-47D-30RA 44-33010 L3-G.

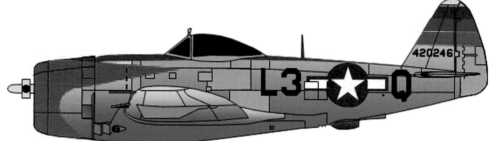

Ernie Sprouse's 44-20246 L3-Q was also brand new on February 22, when the 512th and 514th squadrons clashed with a large force of German aircraft. The many brand new Thunderbolts gave a good showing against the Germans.

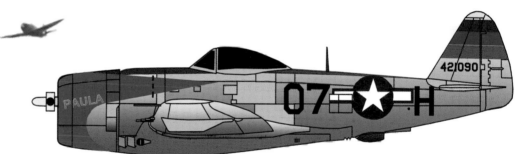

"PAULA." Pilot: 2Lt. Kenneth L. Glemby

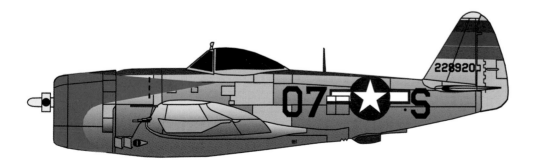

Pilot: 2Lt. Milton Sanders

CHAPTER 15
Patchwork P-47s

The extensive and relentless battle damage caused by murderous German flak and fighters led the 406th FG depot and unit maintenance teams to replace damaged components, when possible, with parts from the large boneyard of aircraft too badly damaged to repair. This led to many odd mismatches in paint, and some very colorful P-47s.

This 512th FS P-47D-11RE has bare metal rudder and horizontal stabilizers on an otherwise (except for bare-metal patches) OD/gray plane.

Canopy frames, cowling panels, and gear doors were easily and frequently replaced. *All photos this page courtesy of Pima Air and Space Museum*

This late-model bare-metal 513th FS P-47 has an olive-drab-and-gray left wing.

This late-model bare-metal 514th FS P-47 has an olive-drab-and-gray left wing. *Courtesy Pima Air and Space Museum.*

Replacement side cowling panel

Replacement lower cowling panel and olive-drab-and-gray left wing, *Courtesy Pima Air and Space Museum.*

Ailerons and flaps were also easily replaced. *Courtesy Pima Air and Space Museum.*

"Miss Lace" with olive-drab-and-gray cowl flaps and gear door. Her feet were lost with the bare-metal cowl flaps. *Courtesy of Pima Air and Space Museum*

Number 5 on replacement bottom cowling panel identifies this part as coming from another unit. *Courtesy of Sprouse family*

Replacing cowling panels was easy, but this olive-drab-and-gray P-47 also has bare-metal cowl flaps.

The 512th FS mascot, "Andy," on olive-drab-and-gray horizontal

CHAPTER 16
Angie

The Plane on the Stamp

P-47D-27-RE 42-26860 was delivered to the USAAF at Farmingdale, New York, on May 24, 1944. It was placed on a ship sailing for England almost immediately, arriving on June 10, 1944. It appeared in full D-day markings and was coded L3-G in two photos at right, taken at ALG 417, Ashford, Kent, UK, in July 1944. The commander of the 406th Fighter Group, Col. Anthony V. Grossetta, is posing with the aircraft in these two photos; the 512th FS maintained his aircraft throughout the war, and "high rollers" such as him usually were assigned the aircraft ID letter corresponding to their last name, so it is likely that this was his assigned aircraft at the time of the photo. The plane was delivered with a Hamilton Standard Hydromatic paddle-blade propeller, the type shown in the two photos.

By November 1944, the aircraft had been extensively repaired. Photos at the top of the next page show that it had a replacement right wing and empennage, taken from older olive-drab-painted P-47s. The plane in the background of the photos, 42-28918, crashed and was totally destroyed on December 2, 1944, so the wing and tail repair occurred before that date.

Both photos taken the same day, courtesy of Pima Air and Space Museum

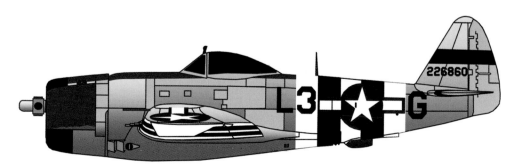

Col. Anthony V. Grossetta. *Courtesy of Pima Air and Space Museum*

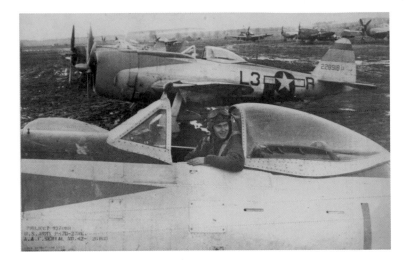

"Angie" January 1945

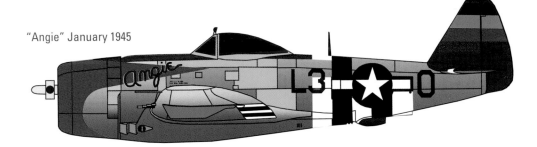

Note that the yellow nose blaze had been painted on 42-26860 by this date, but that the name "Angie" had not yet been applied. The stripes of the group marking had also been painted on the vertical tail. Note in both photos that the fuselage invasion stripes have been only partly removed, and the olive-drab antiglare panel aft of them is missing. Perhaps the fact that the antiglare came off with the stripes is the reason the process was aborted.

A later photo, showing 1Lt. Walker Diamanti in front of the plane on a snowy background, was obviously taken in late December 1944 or early January 1945. In this photo, the name "Angie" has been applied. However, the well-known pinup artwork was not present, and Diamanti stated it was never carried on the plane while it was assigned to him. He also said that he had the name "Angie" painted on the plane to honor a girl he admired back home, but that although they remained friends after the war, they did not marry.

Note in the photo that the Hamilton Standard propeller had been replaced with a Curtiss Electric asymmetric paddle-blade prop.

1Lt. Walker Diamanti. *Courtesy of Pima Air and Space Museum*

Angie at Y-29. *Courtesy of Pima Air and Space Museum*

Lt. Diamanti left Y-29 for the States on January 12, 1945, and, most likely, L3-O was assigned to 2Lt. Fred V. Brandt at that time. On many occasions Brandt stated that he shared the plane with Col. Grossetta, but the colonel was seldom around so he had the plane mostly to himself. From December 6, 1944, to February 23, 1945, Col. Grossetta was on leave, which included thirty days in the US, so Brandt probably had the plane totally to himself from January 12 to February 23. It is likely that the following, most famous photo of L3-O 42-26860 was taken during this time:

In the photo, the name "Angie" is still visible, but the famous pinup is also now in place. It appears that the pinup was added to the aircraft by the simple expedient of replacing the side cowling panel with one on which the pinup had been painted. This panel most likely came from another aircraft, since the squadron's yellow cowling blaze had not yet been painted on it. The plane still has the Curtiss Electric propeller. The replacement horizontal and vertical tail parts, taken from an olive-drab-painted P-47, are clearly visible. The three photos on page **48** show how the replacement parts were probably installed. Note that when the maintainers stenciled the correct serial number on L3-O's replacement tail, they placed the numbers higher than normal, and the number "8" is lower than the others. Also note that no oversize insignia is visible on the underside of the left wing. Perhaps that wing was replaced too!

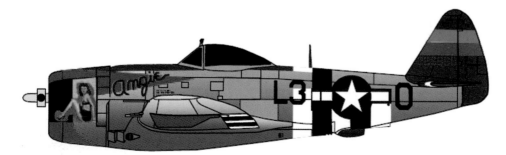

"Angie," February 6, 1945

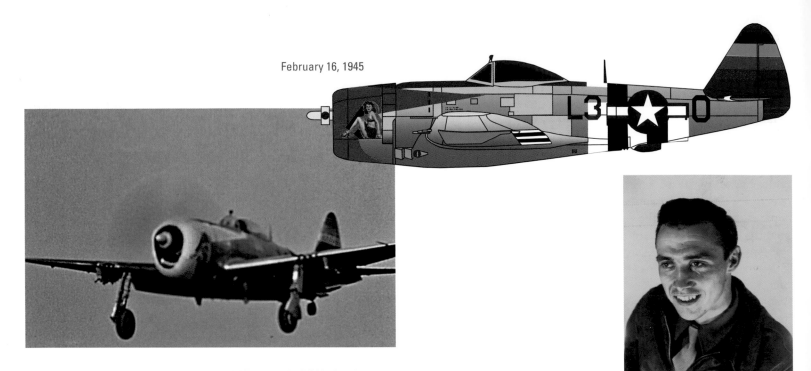

February 16, 1945

42-26860 landing at Y-29. *Digital copy from AAF movie via US National Archives, licensed from criticalpast.com order number 163127912062*

2Lt. Fred V. Brandt

The next photo of interest was extracted from a movie shot by an AAF film crew and apparently is dated February 16, 1945. It shows yet another evolution of the markings on the plane. In this photo, the black ID ring segment of the cowling panel containing the pinup has been painted over in yellow, and the correct outline of the yellow squadron nose blaze has been painted around the pinup to match the rest of the cowling. The name "Angie" is gone.

The olive-drab right wing and empennage visible in the photo eliminate any doubt that this is the same aircraft. In the extensive research performed for this book, no evidence has emerged of any other 512th FS Thunderbolt with this particular combination of replacement parts. Note in the photo that the metal panel covering the gun barrels on the olive-drab-over-neutral-gray right wing is bare metal, and that both the right and left wing pylons are painted neutral gray. Also note in the photo that the black invasion stripe is still visible on the fuselage, above the national insignia. Finally, note that invasion stripes are visible on the underside of the extended left flap, but not on the underside of the left wing. This plane was quite a collection of parts!

If the February 16, 1945, date for the movie is correct, then it is likely that Lt. Brandt is the pilot shown. His logbook indicates

that he flew a combat sortie that day. It is also likely that the changes to the markings were made while Lt. Brandt was the primary pilot. The 406th Fighter Group moved to airfield Y-29, near Asch, Belgium, in early February, with the planes arriving on the eighth. Both the famous photo and the movie were taken at Y-29, so the photo must have been taken almost immediately after the plane arrived. This leaves a few days for the cowling panel to have been repainted in time for the plane's February 16 movie appearance. Significantly, the war diary of the Black Watch (Royal Highland Regiment) of Canada recorded that February 16, 1945, was a sunny day, so the date for the movie is plausible.

Col. Grossetta returned from his leave on February 23, 1945, and the next day Lt. Brandt was wounded during an attack on a marshaling yard near Düsseldorf, Germany. Brandt was not flying 42-26860 that day. An explosion in the marshaling yard threw up debris that shattered his plane's windscreen, temporarily blinding him with glass shards in his eyes. He somehow managed to maintain aircraft control and return for a landing at Y-29. He spent the rest of the war recuperating from his wounds. One can assume that at this point, L3-O 42-26860 was assigned to Col. Grossetta again, and that after Brandt returned to the 512th on May 15, 1945, they shared the aircraft. The aircraft ID code remained L3-O. On May 23, 1945, Col. Grossetta passed command of the 406th FG to Lt. Col. Converse B. Kelly. After that date, Brandt probably once again had the plane all to himself as he served as part of the Allied occupation forces.

Two more photos, both of relatively low quality, give additional details of the markings on L3-O and their evolution. One was taken at airfield Y-94, Handorf, Germany, and the other probably at R-56, Nordholz, Germany. The 406th FG moved to Y-94 on April 15, 1945, and to R-56 on June 8. Of particular interest in both photos are the two stripes, one white and one black, painted over the antiglare panel aft of the cockpit of L3-O. These are apparently remnants of the invasion stripes. Also note the absence of antiglare paint on the fuselage aft of the stripes.

Note in the first photo that the propeller had been changed to a symmetrical paddle blade. This probably happened after a March 9, 1945, "nose-up" accident. Note in the second photo that the squadron code letters, L3, are placed relatively high on the fuselage. The top edge of the crossbar of the *L* is at the panel line between the upper and lower fuselage halves. Most later bubble-canopied P-47s had their national insignias painted higher on their fuselages than the ones on this aircraft. For those planes, the high placement of the L3 caused it to be centered on the horizontal bar of the insignia. For L3-O, on the other hand, the lower placement of the insignia makes the L3 look like it is "riding high."

The second photo, shown actual size, was carried by Fred Brandt in his wallet for fifty-four years. He had better P-47 photos, such as the one of L3-N shown on page 87. He carried this one because it was the only photo he had of "his" Thunderbolt. Though worn and stained from handling and several trips through the washing machine, there is no doubt this photo shows 42-26860 L3-O. It is impossible to tell for sure if the pinup artwork is still present, but the pattern of light and dark areas suggests that it is. The concrete taxiway in the photo indicates it was taken at either Y-94 (Handorf) or R-56 (Nordholz).

Also note in the photo that the rudder shows bare metal, and the plane sports a bare-metal dorsal fin. More parts changes! The dorsal fins were added to all the group's bubble-canopied P-47s starting in February 1945, to prevent an occasional "rudder lock" phenomenon where the aircraft alternated between extreme left and right yaw with the vertical tail stalled. This condition was made possible when some of the P-47s' rear fuselage area was removed when the design was modified to use a bubble canopy. L3-O apparently had received the dorsal fin mod to prevent the stability problem by the time of the final photo. P-47 42-26860 was stricken from 9th AF records on May 23, 1946. Some stories suggest that it and many other P-47s were bulldozed into a pit at R-56.

This photo probably shows the group subdepot at Handorf, since Thunderbolts from all three squadrons are visible. Note salvaged bare-metal wings lying on the grass. *Courtesy of Pima Air and Space Museum*

June 1945

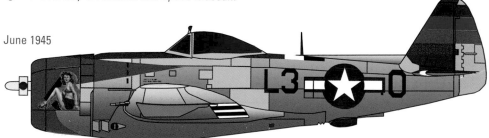

The photos on this page almost certainly show the right side of 42-26860 L3-O. The aircraft named "Patty" in the lineup above has an olive-drab and gray right wing with bare-metal cover over the guns; olive-drab and gray gear door and rudder; low-placed fuselage insignia; proper style, color, and location of mirror; and correct portion of ID code visible. The propeller is now symmetrical paddle blade as confirmed in the photo on page **69.** No research to date has discovered any other 512th FS P-47 with this combination of parts and markings. This is without a doubt 42-26860 L3-O.

According to Ernie Sprouse, pilot of 44-20246 L3-Q "Gladys" / "TEXAS KAY," crew chiefs chose the markings for the right sides of the aircraft noses. This probably started very late in the war or postwar.

June 1945

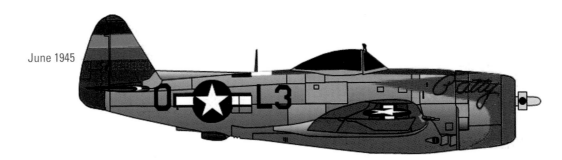

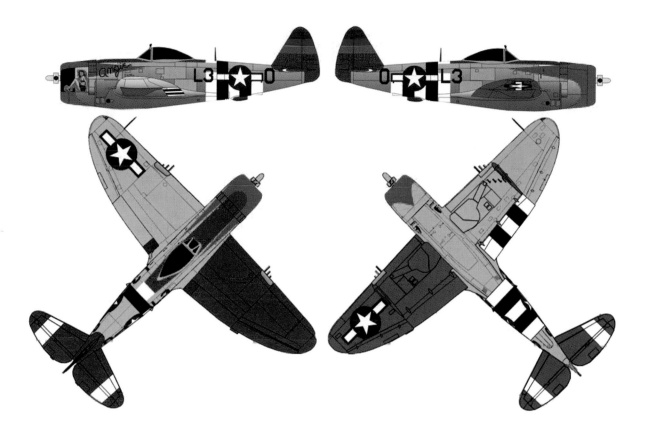

Four-view of 42-26860 L3-O "Angie" as it appeared around February 6, 1945.

This was a truly amazing aircraft. It survived a year of combat because it always returned from every mission, even though it was badly damaged. This allowed maintenance personnel to replace damaged parts with parts salvaged from other aircraft in the 406th Fighter Group's boneyard. The olive drab and gray right wing and empennage were obviously replacement parts from older aircraft.

But the left wing originally appeared with an oversize US insignia on its underside, so it may have also been replaced. The left flap, with its invasion stripes, was probably one of the last parts replaced. The appearance of this aircraft and its longevity are testaments to the brutality of the tactical air war in Europe and the ingenuity of the 406th FG maintenance team.

One of the first scale models made of 42-26860 L3-O was commissioned by the author in 1989 when he was stationed at Clark AB in the Philippines flying F-4 Phantom jet fighters. The only readily available photo of L3-O at the time was the tiny photo carried in Fred Brandt's wallet that is reproduced actual size on page 69. No one noticed the olive drab empennage in that photo and the right wing could not be seen, so the skilled Flipino craftsmen made the model with bare metal wings and tail. They also left off the pinup and name, since Brandt had never mentioned those. The aircraft serial number could not be read in the photo, so the model was delivered with a fictitious one. When Fred Brandt received the model as a Christmas present, his only comment on noticing the serial number was, "I think it was older than that." Indeed it was!

Thanks to the detective work of author and P-47 fan Roger Freeman, the famous color photo began appearing in books and magazines in the 1990s, and it caught the attention of many P-47 lovers. In 1996, the Hasegawa model company released a kit of the P-47. They chose to model L3-O "Angie." Unfortunately, they misinterpreted the famous photo and gave their version of L3-O a glossy black empennage. Since the right wing is not visible in the photo, they assumed it was bare metal. They also placed the L3 code too low on the fuselage and left off the black-and-white invasion stripe segments behind the canopy, since none of those details were visible in the photo. All of these errors were duplicated in 2003, when the Armour model company issued a version of their 11/4848-scale die-cast P-47 painted as "Angie." In addition, Armour assumed that another pinup panel and Angie name appeared on the aircraft's right side. This last error was duplicated by other companies on their ready-made models of Angie, but not by Armour on their 1/100-scale version of the plane or by 21st Century on their 1/32-scale model.

In 2005, a most gratifying honor was accorded 42-26860 when it was chosen to represent all P-47s in the US Postal Service's "American Advances in Aviation" stamp series. The artist correctly omitted a pinup and name from the right side of the plane and also correctly placed the L3 and O high on the fuselage. Unfortunately, he duplicated the other errors in the Hasegawa kit and also placed the fuselage insignia too high on the fuselage. Nonetheless, the painting and stamp are gorgeous, fitting tributes to P-47s in general and L3-O in particular. Fred Brandt, who delivered mail for the US Postal Service for twenty-five years, would have been so proud!

I hope that what you are now reading is a reasonably complete description of the various color schemes worn by 42-26860 during its life. Perhaps setting the record straight is one more way to recognize and honor the plane, the unit, and the men who helped win the war against tyranny. The story is incomplete and contains some conjecture, but it also contains a true flavor of the incredible achievements in which this aircraft and these men participated.

Fred Brandt with a model of L3-O in 1989.

CHAPTER 17
Bloom's Tomb

Unlike P-47 42-26860 "Angie," the aircraft named "Bloom's Tomb" were not one but a total of nine different P-47s! The assigned pilot was Capt. J. C. Van Bloom. A brief chronology of the comings and goings of these planes was assembled by members of the 406th Fighter Group World War II Memorial Association and published on their website. It is reproduced here as the best available reconstruction of what happened:

1	22 Mar. 1944	406th leaves Camp Shanks, New York for Liverpool, England, on HMS *Stirling Castle*
2	4 Apr. 1944	406th Fighter Group arrives at Liverpool, England
3	5 Apr. 1944	406th arrives at ALG 417, near Ashford, England
4	9 May. 1944	406th's first operational mission over France
5	8 Jun. 1944	Lt. Hall made belly landing in "BLOOM'S TOMB" #1. Hydraulic system on left gear failed
6	29 Jun. 1944	Lt. L. C. Beck, flying P47D 42-8473 shot down by Fw 190 in head on pass, MIA. Beck crash landed in enemy territory in France, and was sheltered by members of the French Underground. The plane he was flying that day was "BLOOM'S TOMB II."
7	10 Sep. 1944	Lt. Isham "Ike" Dorsey flying "BLOOM'S TOMB" (probably III), hit by flak and made a belly landing on front line between Americans and Germans, at Louisville, France. Pilot rescued by an American infantry non-com. Returned to squadron two days later.
8	11 Sep.–21 Oct.	No information, written or pictorial, on "BLOOM'S TOMB IV" and "V"
9	22 Oct. 1944	Capt. Noah Lewin-Epstein, flying "R" a P-47D-28 44-19747, on strafing mission of marshalling yard, hit steel pole and tore off 4 feet 8 inches of left wing. Made very hot landing at A-80, Mourmelon, France. Pilot okay, ship dropped off to sub-depot. A photo in SSgt. E. C. Matzel's collection of plane showing damaged wing has notation on back of photo indicating this was "BLOOM's TOMB VI."
10	2 Dec. 1944	Maj. Kelly and Capt. Van Bloom leave for States, for 30 day leave
11	17 Dec. 1944	Lt. Don Dorman, flying "S", a P47D-28 44-20081, which Dorman is positive carried the name "BLOOM'S TOMB," hit by flak; pilot bailed out. Captured by German troops and became POW. If plane was "BLOOM'S TOMB," it was No. VII. Possibly "R" before "S."
12	30 Dec. 1944	Lt. Vincent Pittala, flying "R" a P47D-28 44-19747, MIA. According to eyewitness report of Maj. George Ruddell, who was leading that flight, Lt Pittala was KIA. So "Bloom's Tomb VI" got a new wing at the sub-depot and since 44-20081 had been assigned to Capt. Van Bloom 44-19747 was likely assigned to another pilot.
13	11 Feb. 1945	Gained new ship, P47D-30 44-33182 "R." Sgt. Van Graffeiland's log showed no further record of that plane; it was assigned to Maj. Kelly as O7-Q "SKIRTY BERT V."
14	13 Feb. 1945	Maj. Kelly and Capt. Van Bloom rejoin squadron
15	15 Feb. 1945	Gained new ship P47D-30 44-33087 "R." This happened at Asch, Belgium, and according to photos and written records, this was "BLOOM'S TOMB VIII." Crew chief, John Orr; armorer, J. Richard Bulford; assistant crew chief, Sgt. Glen Pendelton.
16	28-Apr. 1945	P-47D-30RA 44-33353 "R" assigned, probably after June 1945, at R-56, Nordholz, Germany

"After a number of serious accidents had befallen some of the 'BLOOM'S TOMBS,' and enemy artillery and gun fire damaged others—sufficiently to require replacements—the squadron operations officer suggested to J. C. that perhaps he should change the identifying letter R on his plane to some other letter in the alphabet. Such a change might counter the plane's bad luck and since this was a relatively easy change to make, there was little sense in tempting fate. However, J. C. refused to make that change, insisting on holding on to his 'luck of the draw' letter R, and after a while, this matter became a highly sensitive and hotly debated issue. The dispute was finally settled by a compromise . . . Van Bloom allowed a bar to be placed under the letter R, making it R̲."

That allowed 44-19747, which had been "Bloom's Tomb VI," to keep the O7-R ID when it returned to service after its wing was replaced, while Van Bloom was flying "Bloom's Tomb VII" 44-20081, coded O7-R̲. However, it appears that while Van Bloom was on thirty days' leave in the States in December 1944, the DO had his way, because 44-20081 was coded O7-S when it was lost and pilot Lt. Donald O. Dorman Jr. was made a POW on December 17, 1944. Perhaps O7-R̲ was recoded O7-S after Van Bloom left for the States.

Capt. J. C. Van Bloom on the wing of "Bloom's Tomb VII." *Courtesy of Pima Air and Space Museum*

The nine aircraft named "Bloom's Tomb" all were at one time assigned to Capt. J. C. Van Bloom. Most of these carried the ID code O7-R. The O7 code was carried on all 514th FS P-47s, but the plane's identifying letter, R, was assigned by "luck of the draw." In the 512th FS, the aircraft ID letter was sometimes matched to the first letter of the assigned pilot's last name, but not so in the 514th. Van Bloom got the letter R by pure chance.

The 406th Fighter group Memorial Association's website states the following: "The original NOSE ART on 'BLOOM'S TOMB' depicted a pilot in a flight suit, sitting on top of a winged flying coffin, gliding through space—while thumbing his nose (at the enemy, so I'm told). All this against a background of a white, puffy cloud. This same basic design was displayed on eight of the nine planes assigned to J. C. It seems that the artist, SSgt. Sam Mickwee, our squadron intelligence department chief, got just a little tired of repainting the same design, time and time again; feeling certain that in a few weeks, it would only again vanish. Thus, on the ninth P-47D 44-33353, he painted a picture of a tombstone, with that recognizable phrase 'BLOOM'S TOMB' underneath it.

"Bloom's Tomb VII" parked at Y-29. *Courtesy of Pima Air and Space Museum*

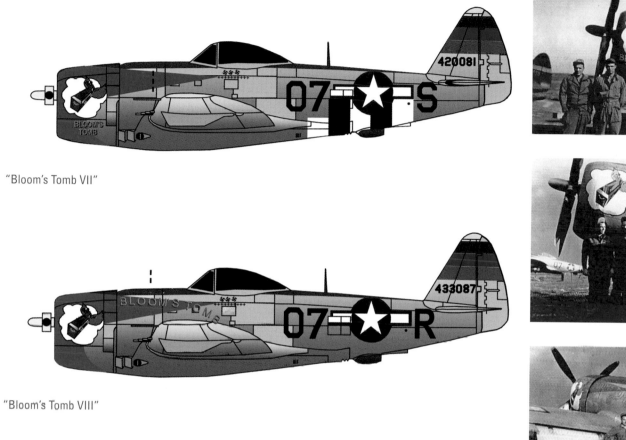

"Bloom's Tomb VII"

"Bloom's Tomb VIII"

"Bloom's Tomb IX"

All photos this page courtesy of Pima Air and Space Museum

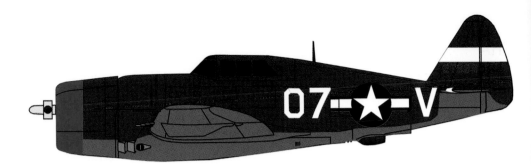

Unlucky O7-V

Not only did the ID O7-R on the nine different P-47s named "Bloom's Tomb" seem to carry with it an unlucky streak, but Thunderbolts with the ID code O7-V also had more than their share of bad luck, at least at landing.

42-7888 O7-V experienced engine failure and crashed at ALG 417 on April 28, 1944. The pilot, Lt. Isham "Ike" Dorsey III, was rescued from the battered wreckage and imminent fire by Capt. George I. Ruddell and SSgt. Alton H. Goad. The rescuers each received the Soldier's Medal for that action.

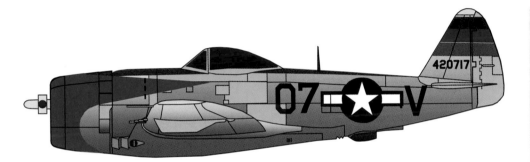

Capt. Bernard Sweet was not so lucky. He perished in this horrific crash of 44-20717 O7-V on March 25, 1945.

Also unlucky, P-47D 42-28859 O7-O damaged beyond economical repair when another Thunderbolt landed on it at Y-29. *Courtesy of Pima Air and Space Museum*

Both photos taken the same day, courtesy of Pima Air and Space Museum

CHAPTER 18
The Rhine

514th FS aircraft undergoing maintenance at Y-29

The month of March 1945 began with a very successful air battle between eight Thunderbolts from the 512th FS and ten Bf 109s and Fw 190s from the Luftwaffe. The Basher Squadron pilots downed five of the enemy and damaged four, without any losses of their own, although one of the credited kills was actually a 109 that shot down another 109!

Then on March 3, the 512th FS had a change in leadership: Lt. Col. Locke relinquished command to Lt. Col. Warren E. Vinzant. Col. Locke was reassigned to XXIX TAC Headquarters. The 512th continued operations with barely any interruption. They flew four missions that day. Then, after six days of bad weather, Col. Vinzant led the first mission of the day on the ninth.

According to the *406th Occupier*, the month of March 1945 "was one of good and constant activity reminiscent of the summer of 1944, with early take-offs and landings around 2100 hours. The sweep to the Rhine and the air power that supported it was clean cut and quick. As it was completed, the group shifted without a halt into the job of aiding in isolation of the Ruhr. Mission after mission was run against the small marshaling yards that form the edge of the built-up area of that great industrial section. Every known method was used to find and destroy profitable targets. Tactical reconnaissance radio broadcasts were monitored for late traffic sightings in the assigned recce area, two ships known as snoops preceded each flight to the target area to find targets, and hot targets were constantly passed from one squadron to the other, both on the R/T and by telephone immediately after interrogation."

On March 14, the 512th FS flew a mission against a marshaling yard near the small village of Brugge, Germany, northeast of Cologne. That day, Lt. Will Cunningham was flying his fifty-eighth combat mission in Lt. Donal G. Whicker's plane, a green-and-gray-painted bubble job coded L3-T and named "Wee Winnie." The plane, 42-26661, had previously served in bare metal with the 352nd FS of the 353rd FG. It is not clear when or how it got painted olive drab or British dark green.

Cunningham, in L3-T, was hit by flak and caught fire. He was at very low altitude and had to climb enough to bail out. The flames from the burning fuel tank came into the cockpit and burned his legs and right hand on the joystick. When he reached 500 feet, he jettisoned the canopy and unstrapped. The change in airflow brought the flames more aggressively into the cockpit, burning his face and neck. He exited the plane as quickly as possible, watched the horizontal stabilizer go by, and then pulled the rip cord. His parachute opened just before he hit the ground.

Cunningham's time under canopy was very short. He almost landed on a young man who was pointing a rifle at him. He was quickly surrounded by a group of farmers with rifles and shovels. They were very aggressive toward him. One burly man repeatedly tried to hit him in the head with a shovel. Fortunately, a German soldier arrived and took him into custody. His burns were very painful.

Crew chief Dale Beerworth and pilot Donal Whicker in 42-26661.
Courtesy of Pima Air and Space Museum

Crew chief Dale Beerworth with "Hank" on 42-26661 *Courtesy of Pima Air and Space Museum*

2Lt. William Cunningham. *Courtesy of Cunningham family*

There followed agonizing days of travel, interrupted at one point by an attack by the red-nosed 513th FS on the train they were traveling in! After that they traveled on foot, with some RAF POWs carrying Cunningham. They eventually arrived at an interrogation facility near Oberusel. From there the healthy POWs went on to a camp, while Cunningham was taken to a Wehrmacht hospital. There he received treatment for his extensive burns. Several soldiers and medical staff treated him with kindness during this time.

Several days later, Lt. Cunningham was moved to a different hospital and received additional treatment. The next morning, he received more treatment for his burns. That evening, the hospital commander came to his room and surrendered the hospital to him!

The commander asked what he should do next. Cunningham told him to have his personnel surrender all their weapons to him and move the other American pilots into his room. By the next morning, he had two new roommates and two large baskets of weapons in his room. The hospital commander's clerk surrendered his own Walther P38 pistol to Cunningham. Will kept that one!

Lt. Edmund Volts. *Courtesy of Cunningham family*

Capt. James C. Brown. *Courtesy of Pima Air and Space Museum*

Early the next morning they heard the rumble of American tanks in the street. The next day they were moved to an American hospital. William Cunningham's POW ordeal was over.

On another 512th FS mission during this time, Capt. James C. Brown's plane was hit by flak. With his engine losing power, he made a belly landing in a large grassy field in enemy-held territory. Lt. Edmond Volts landed his Thunderbolt in the field beside his flight leader. Capt. Brown jumped into the cockpit and sat on Volts's lap. They flew like that back to Y-29. No POW time for Brown!

Another big operation soon followed. From the *406th Occupier*: "On the 22nd of March the group commander, the operations officer, the intelligence officer and the ground liaison officer went to Munchen Gladbach for Command's briefing on the last great air show of the war, Operation Flashpoint. The group's assignment in the air part of this crossing of the Rhine was one of the most difficult jobs ever given it. It called for flak suppression by bombing and strafing and launching of rockets in an assigned area near the Allied airborne landing area. The 23rd of March was spent in planning and preparing for the mission and early on the morning of the 24th,

the day of the operation, the briefing was held. This briefing approached the one for invasion of the Continent in suppressed excitement. It was a well planned and executed briefing. First the ground liaison gave the ground picture as to where and how the crossing would be made, then the intelligence officer outlined the air plan and briefed in detail on the location and capabilities of all known gun positions in the assigned flak suppression area, following which the group commander assigned specific gun positions to each squadron and instructed on the tactics to be used in attacking individual light gun positions as they revealed themselves."

The mission was effectively executed. The group patrolled for over three hours during the drop operation. They silenced particularly intense and accurate fire against the troop transports in the area east of Wesel along the uncompleted autobahn. Unfortunately, Lt. Col. Gordon W. Fowler, 513th squadron commander, did not return from the first mission. This was a particularly poignant loss for the 513th. Their previous acting squadron commander, Maj. Richard D. Graves, had been lost just a month prior, the day before Lt. Col. Fowler returned from leave.

514th FS aircraft undergoing maintenance at Y-29

514th FS aircraft undergoing bomb loading at Y-29

514th FS aircraft undergoing bomb loading at Y-29. *Three-photo sequence courtesy of Pima Air and Space Museum*

The *406th Occupier* continues: "With the crossing of the Rhine the Group turned to affording armored column cover, usually for the Second Armored Division[,] which drove north of the Ruhr toward Munster and out into the open country of the North German Plain. As this drive developed momentum and went into the breakthrough stage, it became necessary to carry external gasoline and fly longer and longer missions to afford the necessary air cover. This period too was marked by a general shortage of bombs and ammunition. We carried anything and seldom did two planes of the same flight carry the same loading, but the air cover was maintained.

"With encirclement of the Ruhr and establishment of the pocket there, we turned again to some in-close ground work but for the first two weeks in April the main job was to sustain the thrust into and across the north of Germany. It was soon apparent to all that we would not be able to continue to fly the exceedingly long missions, which being based in Belgium required, so plans were laid for what many considered the last move."

CHAPTER 19
Handorf

406th FG aircraft undergoing maintenance at Y-94. Note camouflage netting over buildings. *Courtesy of Pima Air and Space Museum*

Y-94, Handorf, Germany
April 15–June 5, 1945

The *406th Occupier* describes the move: "The site this time was the former major German airfield at Handorf, northeast of Munster, now known as Y-94. In the middle of April we reluctantly left Y-29 and came into Germany amid much preparation for security and non-fraternization. We cleared the small village of Handorf near the airstrip and established ourselves in the relative comfort of buildings and homes available there. From Handorf the group's missions were more in the nature of a riot than anything else but for a few days at least the tempo was fast. At the time the 2nd Armored Division and the 5th Armored Division were closing to the Elbe River north and south of Magdeburg, the enemy was being overrun and was exceptionally vulnerable, particularly his aircraft on the ground."

Several airfield attacks during the days just before and after the move to Handorf pushed up the number of claims for aircraft destroyed on the ground. For the month of April 1945, the 512th FS alone claimed sixty-seven enemy aircraft destroyed and twenty-two damaged on the ground in the course of five separate airfield attacks. In like manner, Capt. Milton W. Sanders led the 514th on an attack on an airfield at Celle, Germany, on April 8. They claimed twenty-eight destroyed and fifteen damaged.

In just a few more days, the area in which the 406th could operate dwindled to almost nothing. On April 19, a Russian air boundary appeared between Berlin and the Elbe. This effectively limited group activity to the east bank of the Elbe. On the twentieth they flew a full schedule of ground cooperation missions, none of which were very successful. The following day the unit was put on ground alert. With the junction of American and Russian forces two days later, the job was done.

The group remained on ground alert during the last few days of April and also flew patrol over the Elbe. Group personnel tried to get accustomed to the forced inactivity and impatiently awaited the German surrender and Victory Day. The end came as an anticlimax. The men were content to relax and let events unfold as they would.

One major task completed at Handorf was runway laying. The existing runway was a bit short, so once supplies were collected, the group proceeded to extend the runway by 1,000 feet by laying down straw, tar paper, and then interlocking PSP mats. This was a major task, normally performed by engineers prior to the group moving to an airfield. In this case, it appears the work was done mostly by group personnel. They probably all remembered the bad situation at A-36 and wanted to prevent similar problems at Y-94.

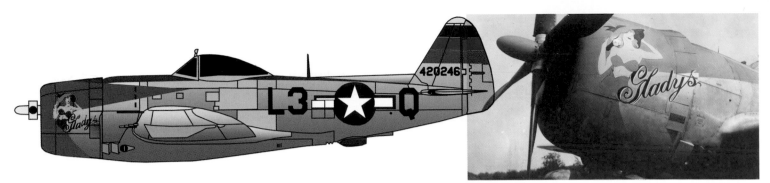

"Gladys." Pilot: 2Lt. Ernie Sprouse. Other side of nose had "TEXAS KAY" painted on by the crew chief.

"Gladys." *Courtesy of Sprouse family*

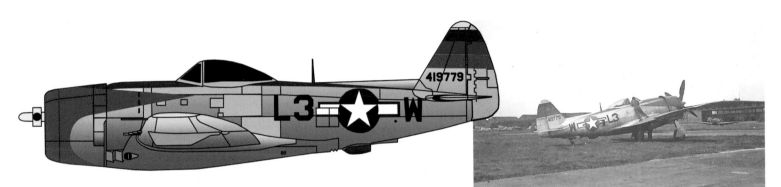

The aircraft assigned to 2Lt. William Cunningham had the ID L3-W, but he was shot down on March 14, 1945, in Whicker's 42-26661 L3-T and became a POW. 44-19779 may have been his plane before that date.

The variety of aircraft and buildings in the background suggests that L3-W is not at its home base in this photo.

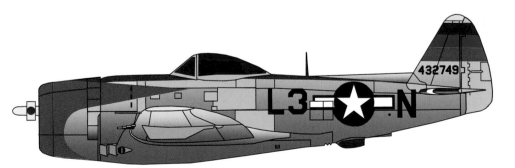

Pilot: 2Lt. George Chin

2Lt. George Chin in 44-32749. Note that horizontal stabilizer is still olive drab.

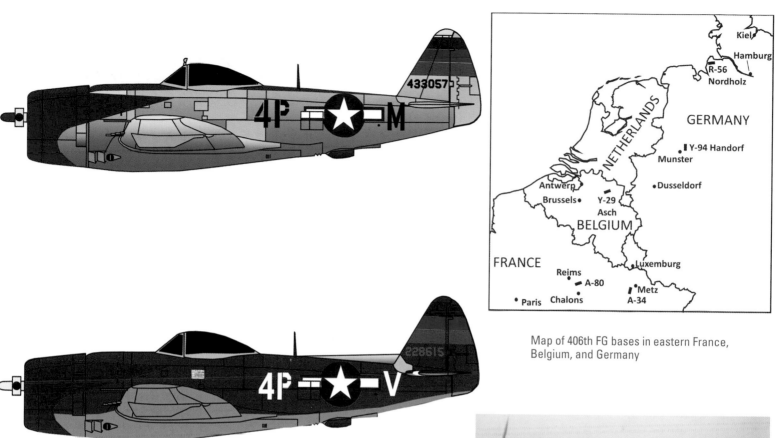

Map of 406th FG bases in eastern France, Belgium, and Germany

Pilot: Lt. Lloyd W. Pearson. Previously, WX-Z "My Baby" in 84th FS, 78th FG.

513th FS aircraft parked at Y-94. *Courtesy of Pima Air and Space Museum*

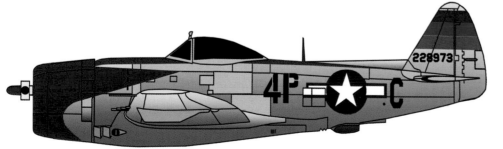

Pilot: Lt. John Bazan. This aircraft had an olive-drab-and-gray right wing.

514th FS aircraft parked at Y-94. *Both photos courtesy of Pima Air and Space Museum*

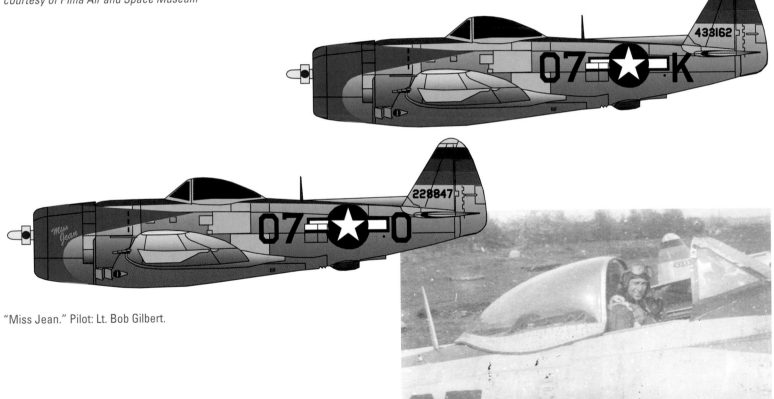

"Miss Jean." Pilot: Lt. Bob Gilbert.

514th FS aircraft ready to taxi at Y-94. *Courtesy of Pima Air and Space Museum*

CHAPTER 20
VE! and Occupation

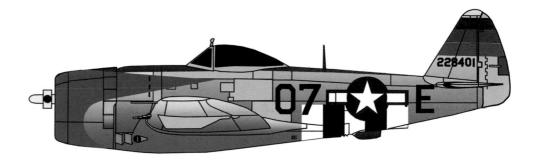

As displayed under the Eiffel Tower as part of the VE celebration

The Nazis surrendered unconditionally on May 8, 1945, one day short of one year after the first combat mission of the 406th FG. A final tally of 406th Fighter Group activity for the period from May 9, 1944, to May 8, 1945, includes 13,612 sorties, 34,000 hours of flying time, 133 P-47s lost to enemy action, 85 men MIA/KIA, 292 enemy aircraft destroyed in the air or on the ground, tons of ordnance delivered, and thousands of targets destroyed as contributions to victory in Europe. In terms of air-to-air victories, the 512th FS led the scoring with thirty-four. The 513th had thirty-three total, and the 514th had fourteen. No pilot became an ace while in the 406th. However, Capt. William Dunn became the first American ace of World War II while flying with the RAF Eagle Squadron in 1941 and then later got one additional air-to-air kill while flying with the 406th. Top scorer in air-to-air kills in the 512th FS was Capt. William Anderson Jr., with 3.5, while Capt. Arner M. Douglas and 1Lt. Donal Whicker both had three. Top score in the 513th FS was shared by 1Lts. William B. Cobb, Raymond R. Stewart, and Elton V. Kern, with three each. Maj. George I. Ruddell was top scorer in the 514th FS, with 2.5 kills. In early 1945, Capt. Rolland Funk of the 513th FS was the top-ranked tank buster in the 9th Air Force, with twenty-two confirmed tanks destroyed.

These 406th officers are relaxing post-VE-day. *Courtesy of Pima Air and Space Museum*

After VE-day, the 406th quickly transitioned to enjoying the relaxed life of members of the Army of Occupation. After the daily stress of combat, the relaxation bordered on boredom. When interviewed many years later, those involved didn't remember much about that time except for one incident. They all remembered that incident vividly and very consistently. The story was inevitably told with great relish in each interview by those who were there.

The incident had its origins when Lt. Gen. William Simpson, commander of 9th US Army, decided to stage a review for the commander of the Russian army across the Elbe River at Magdeburg. Col. Dyke Meyer, XXIX TAC operations officer, called Col. Grossetta three days before the show and asked that the 406th practice spelling out the letters USSR and CCCP with aircraft flying in formation so they could fly that as part of the review.

Col. Grossetta agreed eagerly, and the group put up thirty-six aircraft to practice for the next two days. They formed into four flights of nine aircraft each, one flight for each letter. By the end of the second day, they could fly a pass with the four flights line-abreast spelling "USSR," make a 180-degree turn within sight of the audience on the ground, and fly another pass in the opposite direction, spelling "CCCP." This was precision flying at its best, and the airmen were very proud of their achievement.

Then, on the day before the review, someone from XXIX TAC HQ called to ask the 406th to fly their formations over the headquarters at Braunschweig that afternoon. *If it was good enough*, they would be allowed to fly it for the Russians. Needless to say, Col. Grossetta was very miffed and let the others in the group know it! For the rest of the day, the aerial review pilots practiced another word.

When the appointed hour arrived, the 406th flew over TAC HQ first, with the four flights line-abreast and each in a V formation. As they turned around after the pass, they shifted to "USSR" for the next pass. They turned around again after that pass while shifting to "CCCP" and made their third pass. Then, as they turned around for their final pass, they formed another four-letter word that began with "S" and ended with "T"! They flew that final pass gleefully and with great precision. They wanted to make sure XXIX TAC got the message!

XXIX TAC allowed the 406th to fly in the review but held their breath the entire time, fearing they might be so indiscreet as to insult the Russians. P-47 designer Alexander P. de Seversky, who witnessed the practice flight over XXIX TAC HQ, told Col. Grossetta in 1948 that it was the funniest thing he had ever seen!

Photo from AAF film crew via US National Archives

406TH FIGHTER GROUP BASES		
CODE	NAME	DATES
	Key Field, Meridian, Mississippi	01 Mar. 1943–18 Sep. 1943
	Congaree Army Airfield, South Carolina	18 Sep. 1943–13 Mar. 1944
ALG 417	Ashford, England	06 Apr. 1944–31 Jul. 1944
A-13	Bayeaux, France	31 Jul. 1944–16 Aug. 1944
A-14	Cretteville, France	16 Aug. 1944–06 Sep. 1944
A-36	Le Mans, France	06 Sep. 1944–23 Sep. 1944
A-80	Mourmelon-le-Grand, France	23 Sep. 1944–03 Feb. 1945
Y-34	Metz, France	03 Feb. 1945–08 Feb. 1945
Y-29	Asch, Belgium	08 Feb. 1945–15 Apr. 1945
Y-94	Handorf, Germany	15 Apr. 1945–05 Jun. 1945
R-56	Nordholz, Germany	05 Jun. 1945–20 Aug. 1946

CHAPTER 21
Nordholz

R-56, Nordholz, Germany
June 5–August 1946

Occupying this old Luftwaffe base gave the unit the use of paved runways and taxiways plus masonry buildings.

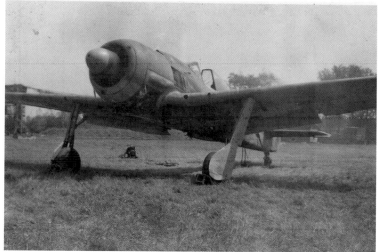

Some German aircraft to "liberate." *Courtesy of Pima Air and Space Museum*

44-32749 parked on edge of concrete taxiway

Courtesy of Pima Air and Space Museum

A 406th FG Thunderbolt makes a low pass as part of an aerial review in honor of a ceremony in which XXIX TAC was presented the "Fourragere 1940" Award by the French minister of defense on July 7, 1945. *Courtesy of Pima Air and Space Museum*

A highlight was the mass flight to Oslo, Norway, on July 4, 1945.

Taxiing for Oslo

All planes carried three drop tanks for this three-hour flight each way.

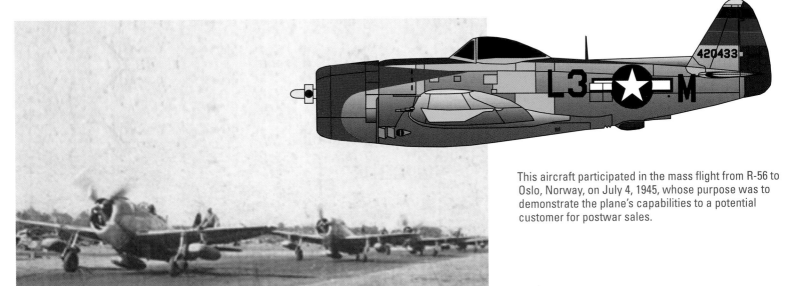

Taxiing for Oslo

This aircraft participated in the mass flight from R-56 to Oslo, Norway, on July 4, 1945, whose purpose was to demonstrate the plane's capabilities to a potential customer for postwar sales.

Courtesy of Pima Air and Space Museum

The 3.5 kill markings identify this aircraft as the one assigned to Capt. William Anderson Jr.

Capt. William Anderson Jr. assumed command of the 512th FS in August 1945. Since the 512th tradition was to assign aircraft ID letters on the basis of the pilot's last name, it is reasonable to assume that L3-A was assigned to him. However, this plane lacks the 3.5 air-to-air kill markings seen on other views of Anderson's plane. Oddly, the nose blaze on this plane is shaped like those on 513th FS P-47s.

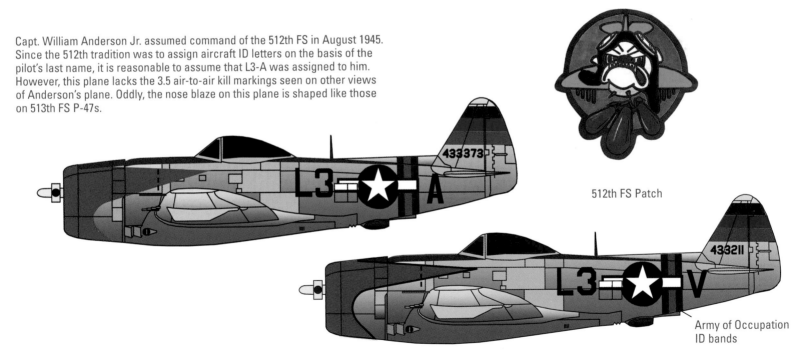

512th FS Patch

Army of Occupation ID bands

On the other hand, Capt. Anderson was flying this aircraft on March 10, 1945, when it was involved in a midair collision with another 512th FS P-47. Anderson landed safely and the aircraft was repaired. When photographed later in 1945, the plane sported the red-yellow-red occupation forces ID bands.

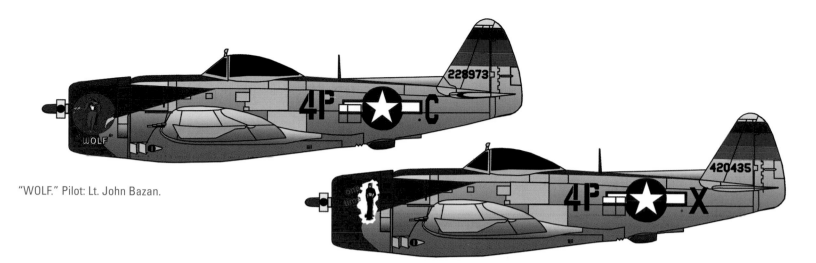

"WOLF." Pilot: Lt. John Bazan.

"One Time." This aircraft came with nose art already applied from 22th FS 36th FG, probably after VE-day.

512th FS Patch

514th FS aircraft parked at R-56.
Courtesy of Pima Air and Space Museum

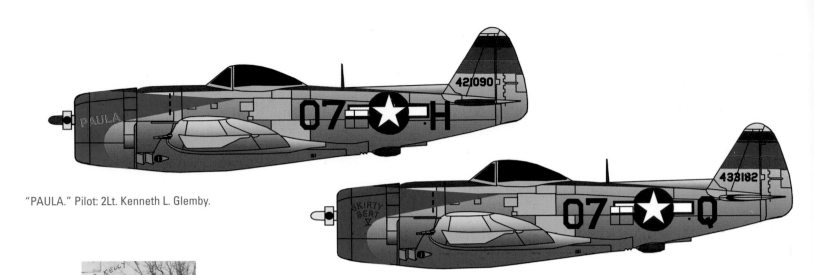

"PAULA." Pilot: 2Lt. Kenneth L. Glemby.

"SKIRTY BERT V." Pilot: Lt. Col. Converse B. Kelly.

Courtesy of Pima Air and Space Museum

514th FS Patch

Courtesy of Pima Air and Space Museum

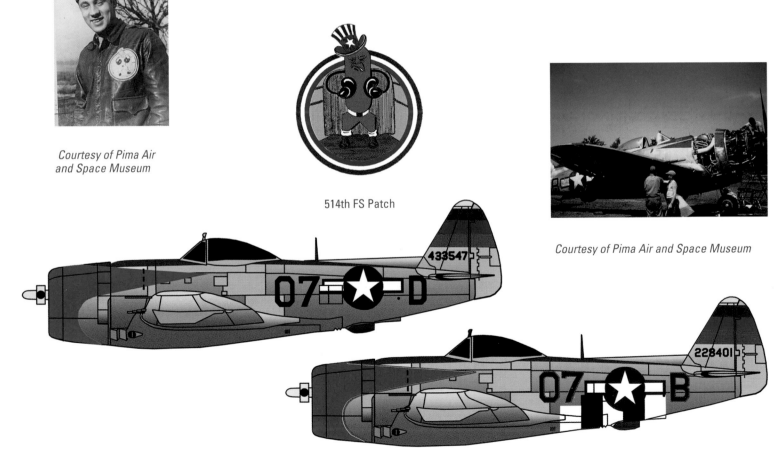

Flying continued after the war ended in Europe. The stated purpose was to "make sure the Germans knew we won the war." *Courtesy of Pima Air and Space Museum*

Another L3-A "Old Buzzard Ass" *Photo courtesy of Sprouse family.*

Some of the black and white film used at the time made the bright yellow noses of the 512th FS P-47s look very dark. Actual color was "slightly lighter than school bus yellow." Red often looked even darker. This photo was taken with a very inexpensive camera that didn't focus well over the whole field of view.

The 512th FS repaired a captured Messerschmitt Bf 108 light civil aircraft and used it as a squadron hack. No captured German fighter planes were flown by 406th FG personnel. All were found to be booby-trapped.

CHAPTER 22
Partials

513th FS P-47 4P-K "Lovely Lou" on takeoff at ALG-417. *Courtesy of Pima Air and Space Museum*

The photographic record is far from complete. It documents only a tiny fraction of the total time and space occupied by the 406th Fighter Group during that year of combat. Up to this point in this book, with a few exceptions, aircraft profiles have shown only those P-47s for which serial number, aircraft ID, and left-side nose art all were known. But in the interest of better capturing the overall appearance, mood, and feel of that year, the next few pages will present aircraft for which only partial information is known. There were so many interesting and attractive paint schemes on 406th FG aircraft with incomplete information that it seems a shame to leave them out.

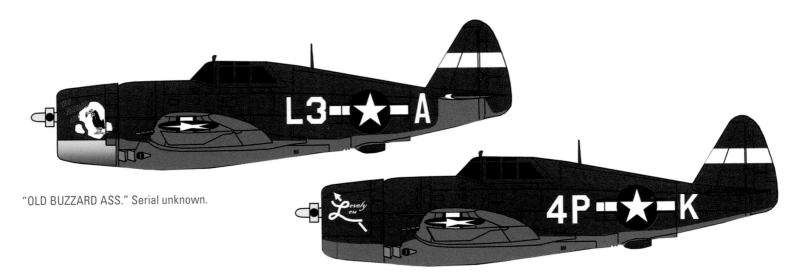

"OLD BUZZARD ASS." Serial unknown.

"Lovely Lou." Serial unknown.

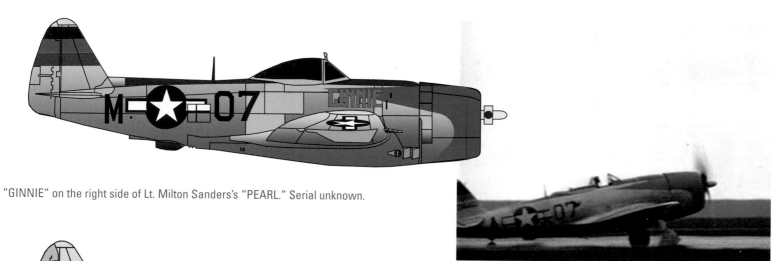

"GINNIE" on the right side of Lt. Milton Sanders's "PEARL." Serial unknown.

514th FS P-47 42-26460 O7-A landing with one main gear wheel missing. *Photo from AAF film crew via US National Archives*

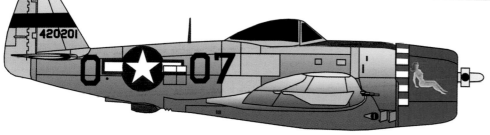

The right side of Lt. Bob Gilbert's "Miss Jean"

Right Sides

Strictly speaking, the information on almost every 406th FG Thunderbolt documented in this book is incomplete. This is because many of those aircraft had different nose art on the right side of the cowling than on the left. In most cases, until very late in the war, there was nothing on the right side, so that is what is assumed for most of this book. But at least at Handorf and possibly before that, some planes had very interesting names and artwork on the right sides.

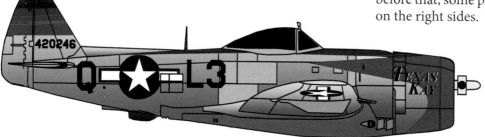

"Texas Kay" on the right side of Lt. Ernie Sprouse's "Gladys"

Right side of Ernie Sprouse's "Gladys." *Courtesy of Sprouse family*

2Lt. George Chin

Courtesy of Pima Air and Space Museum

2Lt. George Chin and 2Lt. Fred Brandt

512th FS aircraft preparing to taxi at Y-29. *Courtesy of Pima Air and Space Museum.*

Unreadable Serial Numbers

Many photographs are of such orientation or poor quality that serial numbers can't be read.

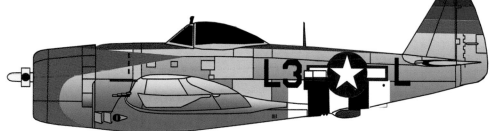

Pilot: Maj. John Locke

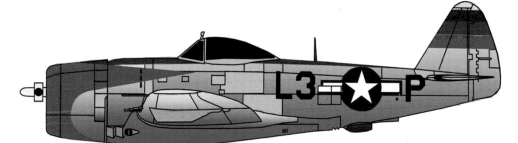

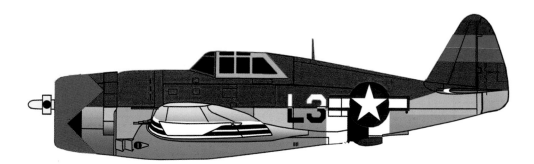

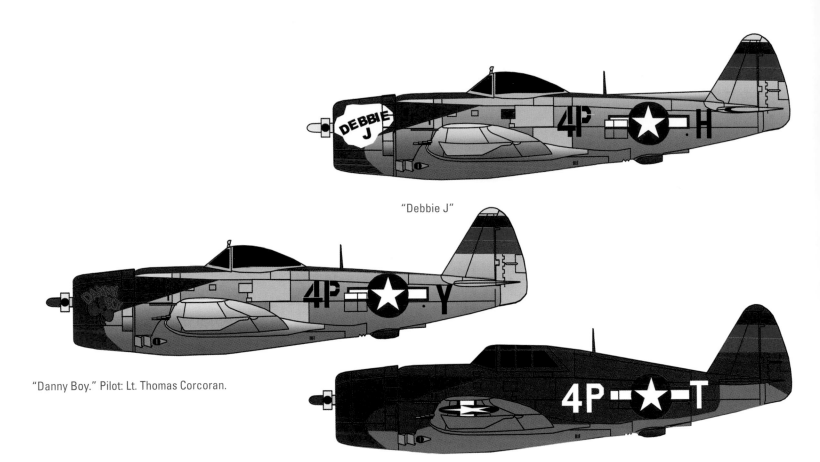

"Debbie J"

"Danny Boy." Pilot: Lt. Thomas Corcoran.

513th FS aircraft parked at
Handorf. *Courtesy of Pima Air and
Space Museum*

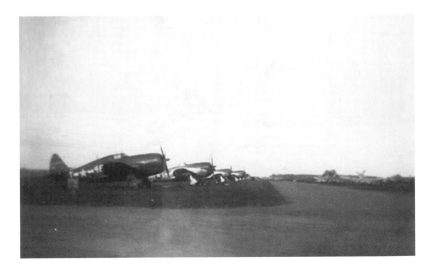

514th FS aircraft parked at Handorf. *Courtesy of Pima Air and Space Museum*

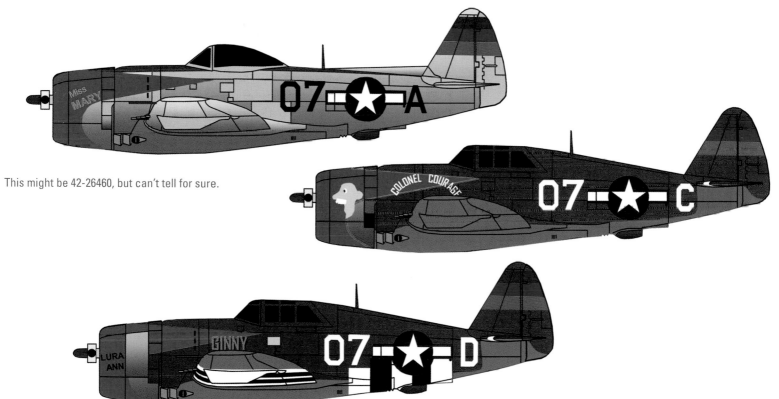

This might be 42-26460, but can't tell for sure.

The red propeller hub on some 514th P-47s probably denoted a particular flight within the squadron.

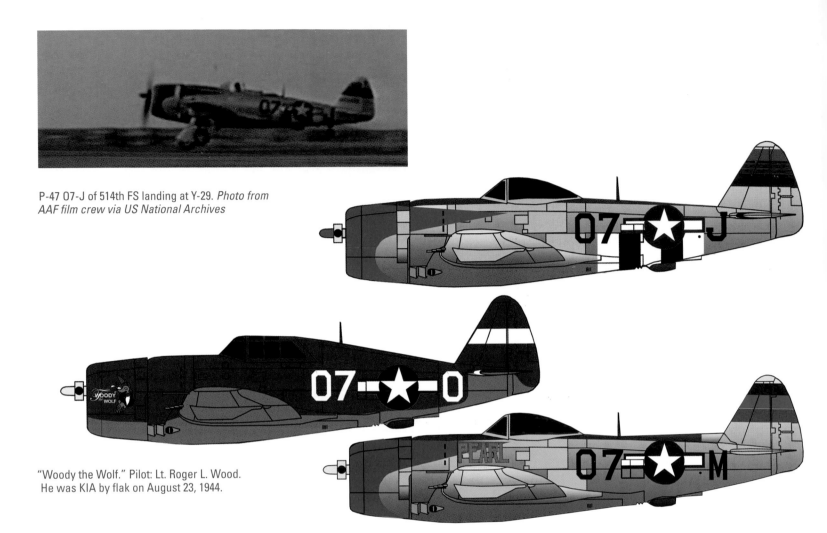

P-47 07-J of 514th FS landing at Y-29. *Photo from AAF film crew via US National Archives*

"Woody the Wolf." Pilot: Lt. Roger L. Wood. He was KIA by flak on August 23, 1944.

"PEARL." Pilot: Lt. Milton Sanders.

"Woody the Wolf"
Courtesy of Pima Air and Space Museum

Some of the 406th's first Thunderbolts in 1943. *Courtesy of Pima Air and Space Museum*

P-47 L3-X of 512th FS taking off

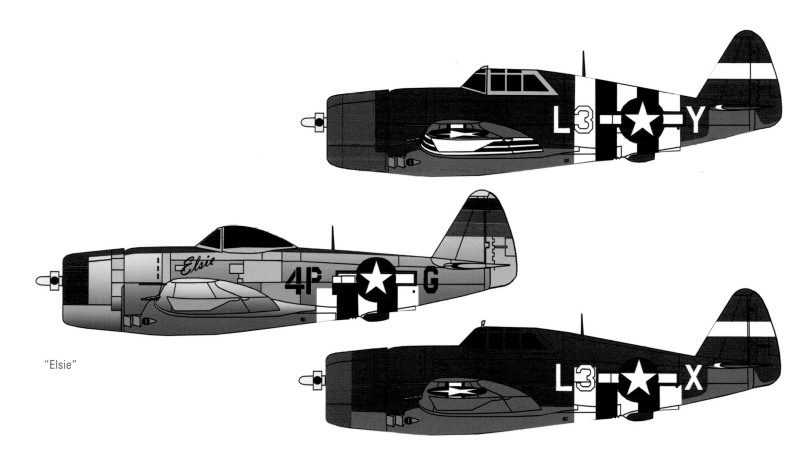

"Elsie"

1Lt. Fred Brandt on cowling over pinup.

1Lt. James C. Brown with crew and "Lillian 2nd" *Courtesy of Pima Air and Space Museum*

Left and above: *Courtesy of Pima Air and Space Museum*

Belly landing in South Carolina swamp.

Flightline maintenance at Congaree Army Airfield, South Carolina.

Bubbble-canopied L3-S was also apparently painted olive drab over gray. Or maybe this was Donal Wicker's "Wee Winnie" L3-T at another stage in its life. *All photos this page courtesy of Pima Air and Space Museum*

Here a Cletrac winch boom crane is used to raise a P-47's rear fuselage so the guns can be harmonized.

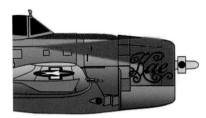

"Kae." Pilot: Lt Robert C. Didier, who later married Kae.

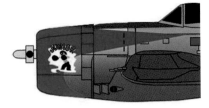

"JUNIOR." Pilot: Lt David R. Eldridge. Aircraft had OD/gray left wing.

Noses

Many photos show only the noses of P-47s. These great works of nose art must be included!

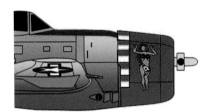

The solid-color cowling and half cowl flaps color scheme was relatively rare on late-model P-47s in the 406th, limited to just a few planes in the 512th and 514th Fighter Squadrons.

"THE BANANA"

Courtesy of Pima Air and Space Museum

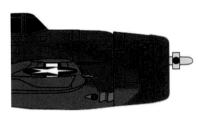

No photos seen to date show a 513th FS P-47 with nose art on the right side.

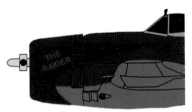

"THE RAIDER." Pilot: Lt Bill Manos.

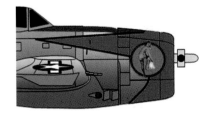

Painting is a more risqué version of a Gil Elvgren pinup.

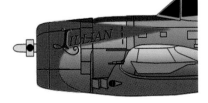

"LILLIAN." Pilot: Capt James C. Brown.

"LARD ASS"

CHAPTER 23
The Nose Blaze

Courtesy of Pima Air and Space Museum

Variously known as the "flash" or "blaze" or "pennant" or "scallop," the stylized shape painted on the cowling and forward upper fuselage of 406th Fighter Group P-47s was unique in history. Other 9th AF fighter units had elaborate shapes painted on their noses, but none quite like the blaze of the 406th. Because it was not painted on every aircraft by the same person, the exact shape of the blaze varied from squadron to squadron and from plane to plane. The drawing on this page shows a standard for the shape commonly seen in the 512th and 514th Squadrons.

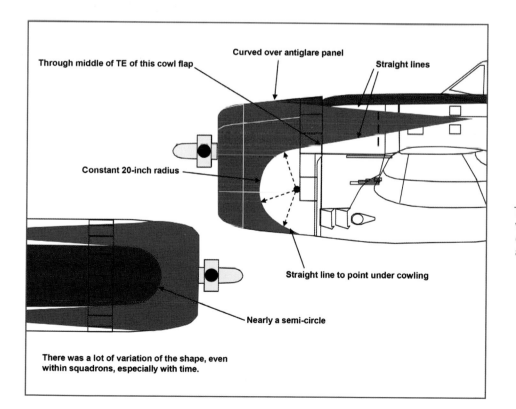

Through middle of TE of this cowl flap

Curved over antiglare panel

Straight lines

Constant 20-inch radius

Straight line to point under cowling

Nearly a semi-circle

There was a lot of variation of the shape, even within squadrons, especially with time.

There were a lot of variations of the shape, even within squadrons, and especially over time.

The 513th FS adopted a slightly different shape for the blaze, bringing it down lower on the cowling, sharpening the lower curve, and squaring off the area over the anti-glare panel. There was also more variability in the blaze shapes in the 513th, especially in the shape of the curve on the lower half of the cowling side panel. Some of these came to a very sharp point with little curve.

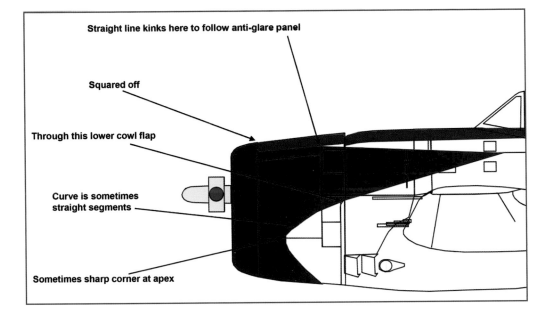

Straight line kinks here to follow anti-glare panel

Squared off

Through this lower cowl flap

Curve is sometimes straight segments

Sometimes sharp corner at apex

Courtesy of Linda Martin

Courtesy of Linda Martin

CHAPTER 24
Propellers

42-26460 with Hamilton-Standard propeller in 1944.
Above and two below courtesy of Pima Air and Space Museum

42-26460 with Curtiss Electric propeller in 1945.
Photo from AAF film crew via US National Archives

Several P-47s delivered to the 406th FG with Hamilton Standard propellers appear later with Curtiss Electric paddle-blade propellers. Why? A story by Jack Bronson may give at least one reason. In May 1944 he was assigned a relatively new P-47D-22 that was equipped with a Hamilton Standard propeller. The plane had good performance, but the prop kept running away. He tried lots of fixes, but to no avail. Finally, Bronson flew the plane to the depot at Burtonwood. In half a day they replaced the prop and governor with Curtiss Electric. No more propeller problems after that! It appears that this same modification was performed on nearly all the Thunderbolts received by the 406th that were originally equipped with Hamilton Standard propellers. Indeed, the vast majority of photos of 406th FG aircraft in 1945 show Curtiss Electric props. The few that show Hamilton Standard all were probably new arrivals or Jugs received from other units after the war. Oddly, most restored P-47s in modern days use Hamilton Standard propellers. For example, the P-47D-40-RA 45-49385, which was restored by WestPac Restorations with a Curtiss Electric prop, now is sporting a Hamilton Standard. The reason given is the much-greater availability and lower cost currently of Hamilton Standard props and parts.

42-26860 with Hamilton Standard propeller in 1944

42-26860 with Curtiss Electric propeller in 1945

Propellers, Nose-Ups

The other most common reason for changing a P-47 propeller was what was called a nose-up or nose-over accident. Taxiing a P-47 had more risks than lack of forward visibility. If brakes were applied too hard or the aircraft hit a small obstruction, the momentum of its 2,400-pound radial engine mounted 8 feet above and 6 feet ahead of the main landing-gear point of contact with the ground would overcome the weight of the Thunderbolt's rear fuselage and the aircraft would face-plant. Such an accident always required a propeller replacement and frequently a new lower cowling. The aircraft in the photos at right are from the 513th and 514th Squadrons, but the official 512th FS unit history for November 25, 1944, states, "Lt Downey nosed his plane over and ruined the propeller but was not injured. It happened while he was preparing to take off on the first mission." Likewise, 42-26860 experienced a nose-up after landing on March 9, 1945.

44-33000 4P-I strayed slightly off the taxiway at R-56 in February 1946, and tripped on a small pile of dirt. *Photo courtesy of Linda Martin*

Aftermath of a nose-over accident. A propeller change was always required.
Courtesy of Pima Air and Space Museum

Propellers, Nose-Overs

The term "nose-over" could also refer to a much more dangerous and often-deadly accident, essentially a nose-up gone too far. If the nose-up happened at too high a speed, especially in mud, the nose would dig into the ground and the aircraft would pivot up and over, ending up inverted. If the plane sank too far into the mud, the pilot could suffocate. It was this type of accident that Lt. Fred Brandt was trying to avoid when he ground-looped his damaged P-47 at the end of his emergency landing roll at Y-29 on February 24, 1945. The photo at right shows a March 14, 1945 nose-over accident at Y-29.

Photos courtesy of Peter Celis collection

GROUP COMMANDERS

Colonel Anthony V. GROSSETTA
Assumed Command 6 November 1943
relieving
Lt. Colonel Bryant B. Harper.

Lt. Col. Leslie R. BRATTON
Became Deputy Group Commander
6 November 1943
succeeding
Captain Samuel R. Beckley.

Lt. Col. Converse B. KELLY
Assumed Command 23 May 1945
relieving
Colonel Anthony V. Grossetta.

Major Clarence H. DOYLE, Jr.
Announced Deputy Group Commander
27 May 1945.

Page 3 from 514th yearbook

The 512th and 514th Squadrons published yearbook-style soft-bound histories of their units for their members to keep and send to family members to help them communicate and remember their experiences during that year of combat. Years later, members of the World War II 513th FS created a similar document and distributed it at one of the reunions.

The 406th Fighter Group published a newspaper called the *406th Occupier* for several months during its service with the Army of Occupation. This served typical newspaper functions for the men of the 406th on occupation duty. Issue number 13 of the *406th Occupier*, dated September 28, 1945, was a special historical issue. It told the story of the 406th FG's origins and year of combat, with many sidebars detailing some of the amazing individual experiences and achievements of its members. That *Occupier* issue was an important source of information for this book, since it was a firsthand account of the group's experiences. Other sources included the official histories of the three squadrons, each one kept by the respective squadron's intel officer. In addition, many 406th FG veterans wrote down their memories and shared them at reunions. Some of these are preserved in the 406th FG Archives at PASM.

Yearbooks

Epilogue

Courtesy of Pima Air and Space Museum

The 406th Fighter Group served with the Army of Occupation until August 20, 1946. By then, virtually all the personnel who served in it during the year of combat had returned to the States. The aircraft and personnel assigned to the 406th at the time of its inactivation were taken over by the 86th Fighter Group, in keeping with the Air Force policy of eliminating high-numbered units in preference to low-numbered ones. The 86th soldiered on to become the only active US fighter group in Germany at the start of the Berlin Airlift in 1948.

The men of the 406th who lived that year of combat mostly returned to civilian life after the war. Col. Grossetta became a civic leader in his hometown of Tucson, Arizona. Lt. Col. Locke became a general officer, and others went on to distinguished careers in the United States Air Force. Walker Diamanti joined the US Foreign Service and was the chargé d'affaires ad interim at the US embassy in Libreville, Gabon, when it was established on March 20, 1961.

The men mostly lost touch with each other over the years, though a few contacts were preserved. After thirty years, Jack Robinson, who had served in the 512th FS, decided he wanted to reestablish those old associations. He began contacting his old squadron mates, starting with the addresses listed in the squadron yearbooks published at the end of the war. In 1981 he led the group's first reunion in Arlington, Texas. Ironically, one of the pilots whom Robinson had been unable to track down, Donal Whicker, lived in Arlington! Whicker learned about the reunion after the fact, when an article about it appeared in the local paper. He attended the next reunion, which was also held in Arlington.

The reunions continued, and the 406th Fighter Group World War II Memorial Association was established as a nonprofit organization dedicated to preserving and honoring the memories of those who fought and those who died during that year of combat. The association established a website, which still operates, and in 2008 they opened a magnificent display at the Pima Air and Space Museum (PASM) in Tucson. The association also established an archive at PASM, to which many members sent their records, photos, and mementos. It is this archive that provided the bulk of the photos for this book.

The final reunion was held in 2007. Most of the men are now gone. Enough cannot be said about what these men did. If this book has helped preserve their memories, it has served its purpose.